VIRGIL

VIRGIL

Jasper Griffin

Bristol Classical Press

To Julia, Miranda, and Tamara
Filiabus Dilectissimis

This impression 2002
Second edition published in 2001 by
Bristol Classical Press
an imprint of
Gerald Duckworth & Co. Ltd.
61 Frith Street, London W1D 3JL
Tel: 020 7434 4242
Fax: 020 7434 4420
inquiries@duckworth-publishers.co.uk
www.ducknet.co.uk

First published in 1986 by Oxford University Press
© 1986 by Jasper Griffin

A catalogue record for this book is available
from the British Library

ISBN 1 85399 626 2

Printed and bound in Great Britain by
Antony Rowe Ltd, Eastbourne

Cover illustration: based on *The Fire in the Borgo* by Raphael,
ca. 1514. Stanza dell'Incendio, Vatican

CONTENTS

Abbreviations

The following abbreviations are used in reference to Virgil's works:

A *Aeneid*
E *Eclogues*
G *Georgics*

Chapter 1

Life and times:
the unity of Virgil's work

Publius Vergilius Maro, in English normally called Virgil, was a celebrity in his own lifetime. His are the first poems in the history of Latin literature to have been the subject of lectures by a contemporary teacher; on his rare appearances in Rome he was pointed out in the street and in the theatre. Consequently there was a great deal of interest in him and writing on the man and his works began early. Yet in life he seems to have been a shy and elusive figure, very different from his friend the urbane Horace. We have much less solid information about him than the considerable volume of ancient *Lives* would appear to suggest.

He was born in a small town near Mantua; 15 October 70 BC is given as his birthday. His family appears to have been respectable but not at all grand. He received a good education at Cremona and Rome but was not, like the rich freedman's son Horace, sent to Athens for those studies in philosophy which for the Roman upper class served as the equivalent of a sojourn at a university. We now think of Mantua (modern Mantova) as an Italian city. In the first century BC, however, it was part of Cisalpine Gaul ('Gaul on this side of the Alps'). The area was thoroughly Roman-ised but it was only in 49 BC, when Virgil was twenty-one, that after long agitation it received the Roman citizenship from Julius Caesar. That astute politician, embarking on a civil war, conferred the cherished status in order to win over to his side the people of a wealthy and populous area.

The civil war between Caesar and Pompey was only one of the self-inflicted wounds which Rome and Italy suffered during the poet's lifetime. In 63, when Virgil was just seven years old, Catiline, at the head of an Italian army, fell fighting in a pitched battle against Roman legions. The 50s were a decade of mounting disorder, during which riots in Rome at times paralysed the processes of government. Caesar, having defeated the Pompeian armies in three years of battles from 49 to 46, was then assassinated on the Ides of March, 44 BC; and another round of civil wars followed. The eventual defeat of Brutus and Cassius and the ascendancy of Mark Antony and Octavian, Caesar's heir, was accompanied by proscriptions, murders, expropriations. A third civil war in 31 BC between Octavian and Antony (with Cleopatra on his side) was necessary before the final victory of Octavian, who returned to Rome in 29 and in 27 took the new name by which he is known to history – Augustus. Of Virgil's fifty-one years twenty-nine were years of war, including sixteen of civil war. In the proscriptions of 42 and 41 it was estimated that at least 150 senators and 2,000 members of the next social class, the equestrians (*equites*), lost their lives; great areas of Italy were devastated by fighting, by famine and by forcible expropriation of land, in which Mantua was heavily punished. Our limited sources inform us of the names of more than fifty suicides in this terrible period.

It was in such a time that the poet grew up. It had begun to look as though the empire won over centuries might finally come to nothing, the Capitol look down on the slaughter of citizens and the end of Rome. The earliest poems of Horace, written in the early thirties BC, include some which express bitterness and despair for the future. Such despair and also desperate hopes for deliverance, sanity, the restoration of the greatness and security of Rome – those feelings are of high importance for the poetry of Virgil, taking various forms in his successive productions. In making himself a mouthpiece for such wide-spread emotions he turned his back on the ideals of the previous generation of poets. For Catullus and his friends prided themselves on their élitism, on their superiority to the ideas and tastes of the bourgeoisie, and on an ostentatious contempt for politics. 'I have no wish at all to please you, Caesar; I don't care whether you are black or white.' So wrote Catullus of the greatest political figure of his age. The output of Catullus and his friends (the Neoteric or New Poet's [*novi poetae*]) fell into two classes: on the one hand short and personal poems, which might be scurrilous squibs, passionate lyrics or versified jokes; and on the other fairly substantial works – 400 lines or so – of exquisite polish on remote mythological subjects, like Catullus' Poem 64, *Peleus and Thetis*, and the recherché *Zmyrna* of his friend Cinna, which required a commentary as soon as it appeared. Outside that group of writers – and as far as we know an isolated figure – stood the great poet Lucretius, whose long poem *On the Nature of the Universe* expounded and passionately advocated the philosophy of Epicurus.

When Virgil began to write, poetry at Rome might well have seemed hopelessly fragmented. The two sides of the output of the Neoteric circle seemed to leave no place for the considered expression of serious thought on central and contemporary subjects, while the grand utterance and poetic power of Lucretius were placed at the service of a philosophy which detached men from politics and the state. Personal emotion, technical refinement, the grand style – all were going in different directions, while the role of expressing and elevating the moral and political ideas of the community, the role performed in Greece by Homer and the Attic tragedians, seemed to be beyond the power or even the desire of Rome's poets. It will provide a key to the career of Virgil if we see him as responding to a crisis both in politics and in poetry. It was the task of the poet to articulate the feelings of his people but the situation of poetry made that task extraordinarily difficult. Catullus, Cinna and others had, by careful craftsmanship and scholarly application, developed a poetic style of great refinement and beauty; but it seemed that in this style nothing could be written but mythological poems with virtually no contact with contemporary life. The refinement of the style, in which the Latin language had at last attained a beauty which stood comparison with the splendours of Greek verse, could not simply be abandoned. A great poet could not go backwards from that achievement. But the vivid reality of Catullus' short poems and the passionate sincerity and depth of thought of Lucretius must somehow be expressed in a style which lost none of the ground gained, in rhythm and euphony, in those exquisite vignettes from Greek mythology.

In the late forties BC Virgil was working on a book of pastoral poems, the *Eclogues*. He proclaims that he is following in the tradition of Theocritus. It is important, not only for the *Eclogues* but also for Virgil's other poems, to understand what is meant by such a claim. Theocritus, a Greek from Syracuse who spent much of his life in the Eastern Mediterranean, in the great city of Alexandria and on the Aegean island of Cos, was writing poetry about 280-260 BC. He was a literary man, whose varied poetic output included works in different dialects of Greek, some of which are in the manner of much earlier poets: several, for instance, are in the dialect and metre of Alcaeus, who wrote on the island of Lesbos three hundred years earlier. That is an indication of Theocritus' approach to poetry: he was by no means an artless rustic himself, however much some of his poems evoke rustic artlessness.

That part of his output which made him celebrated was his 'bucolic' or 'pastoral' poems. These were 'mimes', short sketches (100 lines or less) in a dramatic form which could permit performance – little scenes from the life of rustic herdsmen, who, as they minded or neglected their flocks, talked and sang of love, of the beauties of nature, and of the power of music. Shepherds do have leisure and they often sing: from King David to the Old English Caedmon there is in fact a connection between shepherds and song. But Theocritus makes his rustics sing in a style very different from that of anything which might have been heard on the lips of real Sicilian herdsmen. The poems are in hexameters, the stately measure and long line (thirteen to seventeen syllables) of Homer – a metre equally remote from the rhythm of normal speech and from the short stanzas of folk song. A deliberately cultivated incongruity was part of the aesthetic effect aimed at, when Theocritus versified in hexameters the trivial tasks and amours of his rustics. The mixture was completed by the poet's choice of a subtly different dialect from the Homeric one which was expected as a matter of course from any writer of hexameter verse. An artificial and carefully judged Doric allowed the poet to beautify his poems with long $\bar{o}$ and $\bar{a}$ sounds, musical in themselves and especially delightful because piquantly surprising in the hexameter. Careful attention to rhythm and sound-patterns made the poems hauntingly melodious; and the rustic speakers are characterised as simple yet refined, at once less complex and more poetical than the city-dwelling reader, who is meant to feel both a certain superiority and a certain envy of these simple souls, with so few cares but love and song. The Greekless reader can perhaps get a better idea of Theocritus from some of Tennyson's poems than from an English translation of the original:

> Come down, O maid, from yonder mountain height:
> What pleasure lives in height (the shepherd sang)
> In height and cold, the splendour of the hills?
> ...So waste not thou, but come: for all the vales
> Await thee; azure pillars of the hearth
> Arise to thee; the children call, and I,
> Thy shepherd, pipe: and sweet is every sound,
> Sweeter thy voice, but every sound is sweet;
> Myriads of rivulets hurrying thro' the lawn,
> The moan of doves in immemorial elms,
> And murmuring of innumerable bees.

Theocritus, we have said, was a literary man, one of those patronised by Ptolemy, the cultured king of Egypt, along with other poets, scholars and writers. His elegant poems found imitators in the two centuries between his death and the pastoral compositions of Virgil, and some of those derivative works were accepted by Virgil as original.

Virgil claimed to follow him:

> Prima Syracosio dignata est ludere versu
> nostra neque erubuit silvas habitare Thalia.
>
> (*E* 6.1-2)

> My Muse was the first to feel no shame at sporting in Syracusan verse, nor did she blush to dwell in the woods.

Two questions present themselves: what is the significance of this 'following' of a Greek predecessor; and why does Virgil single out from all of Greek literature Theocritus in particular?

The general question is one of the greatest importance for Latin literature as a whole and it is central not only for Virgil's *Eclogues* but also for his *Georgics* and *Aeneid*. The Romans, a tough and hard-headed people, conquered the world but found themselves confronted by the enormous and undeniable cultural superiority of Greece. In 250 BC the Romans possessed no literature at all, except for a few things like simple songs, formulae and incantations, and a code of law. They found themselves facing the overwhelming splendours of Greek art, philosophy and literature. Paintings and statues could be taken to Rome as loot and soon the city was full of them, but literature was more intractable. The most characteristic strength of Greek art, in all its aspects, was its perfection of form: from the mathematical refinements of the Parthenon to the elaborate exactness of Greek verse and the measured cadences and supple variations of Plato's Greek prose. In the words of Lytton Strachey, 'Greek art is, in every sense, the most finished in the world; it is for ever seeking to express what it has to express completely and finally; and when it has accomplished that, it is content.' On most of the peoples with whom the Greeks came into contact the effect of that formal perfection was deeply demoralising. Lycians, Lydians, Etruscans – they all came under the spell of Greek form; and in most of the languages of the Mediterranean world no literature ever came into existence. Educated Syrians and Cappadocians wrote in Greek; even Jews, Egyptians, and Babylonians – peoples who already possessed literatures before they met the Greeks – began to write in the Greek language. For all those peoples who did not already have literary works of their own, the seductions of Greek form, as well as the possibility which it opened up of an international audience, were too strong. So, in the end, their languages were doomed: Etruscan, Oscan, Messapian, and many others simply withered away.

At the end of the third century BC it began to look as if Latin, despite the conquests of Rome, might go the same way. Roman senators began writing history in Greek; and what created a Latin literature and transformed the Latin language was not the efforts of Roman aristocrats but the work of outsiders of humble position. Latin literature began with a translation of Homer by a Greek slave (Livius

Andronicus); it continued with the work of men who were in no case from Rome itself – Naevius and Ennius from Southern Italy, Plautus from Umbria, Terence from North Africa. It was to turn out that Rome would take a unique course – not that of simple surrender to Greek superiority, nor that of pretending that Greek literature did not exist or presented no problem, but the heroic task of creating in Latin a literature fit to stand beside that of Greece. That meant taking over the Greek forms – epic, tragedy, comedy, history, oratory, lyric – and producing in them works of classic style and stature. We see that Roman literature was the first to go in the direction that was taken, after the Renaissance, by all the literatures of Europe, which in their turn set out to create works in all the classical genres.

For the Romans the struggle was long and arduous. The Latin language seemed to Romans – Cicero, a generation before Virgil, expresses it frankly – less beautiful, less rich, less tractable than Greek. Roman society was in many ways very different from that of the city states of classical Greece. There was always a strong current of philistinism at Rome, which regarded the serious pursuit of the arts as unmanly and absurd, fit only for foreigners who had lost their manhood and their independence through their aestheticism. The Greeks avenged their military defeat and political subjection by rubbing in their unchallengeable cultural supremacy; they regarded with irony or silent scorn the idea that these barbarians might produce anything worth the while of a Greek to read. It was natural that they should feel that; but in the age of Augustus, the time when Latin literature flowered with Virgil, Horace, Propertius, Tibullus, Ovid, and Livy, the Greek world could show no living writers of comparable stature. Naturally they did not admit this; in fact they did not even know it.

When Virgil began to write, the struggle had been in progress for two hundred years. Cicero had been a greater stylist and also a more talented and versatile writer than any Greek of his time, with the one possible exception of the polymath Posidonius. He had produced oratory of a range and power unmatched since Demosthenes, nearly three hundred years earlier. He had 'conquered new provinces for Rome', as he put it in a typically Roman image, by writing philosophical treatises to stand beside those of Plato and literary criticism to rival that of his successors. The Latin language had been enormously enriched by the effort necessary to create the vocabulary for such works. Catullus and the Neoterics had made a close study, including translations into Latin verse, of the works of the most exquisite Greek poets – an exercise that had enriched and extended the range of Latin poetry. But still it was to Greece that Romans naturally looked for the forms of literature. The clear lines and classic quality of the Greek forms so dominated Roman taste that a work of art which did not respect them would have seemed merely barbarous, not recognisable as 'artistic' at all. The strong feelings of Romans needed the supporting framework of Greek models in order to find expression – the obsessive love of Catullus and Propertius, the moral earnestness of Lucretius, the patriotism and pathos of Virgil. It was many years since such powerful emotions had been expressed by Greek writers but, in order to articulate them, the Romans needed the Greek repertory of literary patterns. Virgil would have found a Latin poem with no Greek forerunner unbearably uncouth.

The second question remains: why select Theocritus? In him Virgil found a Greek poet whose work was of a high standard of technical elegance, not yet hackneyed in Rome by any earlier Latin imitators and poised suggestively between naturalism and artifice. Theocritus' herdsmen were clearly something different from what, on the surface, they appeared to be, because of the tension between the subject-matter and the style of their songs. That hint of complexity, implicit in the poems and never explained, offered Virgil intriguing possibilities for handling complex or dangerous material without making his own position explicit or unambiguous. In the next chapter we shall see in more detail how this worked and the highly original and unexpected effects which it made possible, as Virgil introduced specifically Roman elements into the Greek pastoral world.

The *Eclogues* were composed in the years 43-38 BC. What the poet wrote before that we do not know: he did not himself publish and acknowledge anything earlier. There is a curious collection of poems in existence known as the *Virgilian Appendix*, containing a number of things which at one time or another were ascribed to him and which, in fact, survived only because of the protection given by his name. It was the appetite for more poetry by the greatest of Roman poets that led people to accept as Virgilian various pieces, most of which are certainly spurious: some are pastiches of his real works; there is no obvious reason at all to attribute others to him. The only pieces which may really be from his hand are one or two very short poems in a collection of fifteen called *Catalepton (In the Slender Style)*. These are, as one might expect of his earliest productions, very much in the manner of Catullus, the great poet of Virgil's youth. If genuine, they give us tiny glimpses of the poet writing to friends about love, parties and the loss of his Mantuan estate.

The appearance of the *Eclogues* established Virgil as a leading poet. We shall see in the next chapter how he attempted to resolve the great problems of writing them. In the *Eclogues* he addresses a patron, Caius Asinius Pollio, and other great men, as well as friends and poets; but we do not yet find the name of the supreme patron, Augustus' unofficial 'Minister for the Arts', Maecenas. It must have been about the time of the appearance of this, his first book, that Virgil entered Maecenas' circle. It was he who introduced

Horace, another great poet and one of Virgil's greatest admirers. Maecenas presented Horace with an estate in the Sabine country, a piece of land with five tenant farmers on it, which made the poet a man of means. What was done for Virgil we do not know in detail, as he, unlike Horace, did not write autobiographical poems. But ancient scholars who had seen his will tell us that he left the very large sum of ten million sesterces, with substantial legacies to Maecenas and Augustus. No doubt this represented the return of some of the money to its source.

From now on it seems that Virgil lived mainly on the Bay of Naples, in an area of Italy long settled by Greeks (Naples, *Nea Polis*, was an ancient Greek colony) and celebrated for its beauty. His friends there included the Epicurean philosopher Siro, with whom the poet studied. His visits to Rome were infrequent, and he seems to have been a shy and retiring personality. He did not marry.

The year 29 is the traditional and apparently correct date for the appearance of his next poem – the *Georgics*. This time Virgil has gone much further back into Greek literature for a model – not an exquisite and comparatively recent minor master like Theocritus, but the remote figure of Hesiod, regarded as contemporary with Homer. The *Georgics* is a single poem, though divided into four Books. A work of some 2,000 lines is a very great increase in scale from the *Eclogues*, the longest of which has just over 100. The poem is addressed to Maecenas and Octavian (who was himself never mentioned in the *Eclogues* by name) appears in it prominently. By this time the terrible period of the end of the forties was an alarming memory and Octavian had been busy in the thirties conciliating public opinion in Italy and mobilising it against his last rival, Mark Antony. He decisively won the war of propaganda and he was able to present himself as the champion of the Roman West against an enemy who had 'gone native' in Egypt and who planned a shameful Oriental despotism. The battle of Actium in 31 BC involved very little fighting: some of Antony's contingents changed sides at the last moment and the Egyptian fleet sailed away almost without bloodshed. Antony and Cleopatra took their own lives.

At last the civil wars had produced one ruler for the world, just thirty-two years old. What would he do? Anxiety and hope contend in the *Georgics*. As he referred to 'Syracusan verse' in the *Eclogues*, Virgil calls this poem an 'Ascracan song', from Ascra in Boeotia, the home town of Hesiod. The reader is meant to have the pleasure, among others, of seeing how inadequate that description is. The Hesiodic element is much less pervasively present than that of Theocritus in the *Eclogues* but it is among the devices by which the poet can, at will, distance himself from the present, and even from Italy. The poem is 'didactic' —that is to say, it has at least the appearance of a work which conveys instruction. How to recognise good soil, how to choose a horse, what to do if your bees start to fight – there are indeed passages which profess to answer such questions (*G* 2.177ff., 3.100ff., 4.67ff.). But Virgil goes far beyond Hesiod in giving his poem a pervasive moral and reflective colouring: the philosophy of hard work (*labor*) is expounded and traced back to the will of Jupiter himself; the life of the countryman is glorified, transfigured, extolled; patriotic themes of hope for Rome's future and shame for her recent past run all through the poem. The influence of Lucretius, earnest and passionate, is really more important here than that of Hesiod. The *Georgics* are adorned with spectacular episodes of poetry, which Virgil has tried hard to make relevant to his theme. The passages which deal directly with Octavian exhibit a mixture of extreme praise, even flattery, with a certain self-consciousness and an attempt to maintain some distance from what is being said by the use of strange and exaggerated images.

Octavian/Augustus attached great importance to the restoration of a healthy moral climate. The excesses of the last generation – the scandalous exploitation of the provinces, the ruthless individualism which led Roman generals to march on Rome, the spectacular exhibitions of private wealth, the riot of adultery and sexual immorality which seemed to menace the institution of the family – needed to be redressed by a new regime of self-restraint and public spirit. Despite strong resistance, he persevered with a campaign to introduce laws which made adultery illegal, encouraged marriage, limited conspicuous consumption. The poets were evidently under pressure to produce works which would contribute to this moral revival, and perhaps the only poem to be written in response to an actual public commission, the *Carmen Saeculare* of Horace, composed for performance at the Secular Games of 17 BC, duly prays for divine blessing on 'the decrees of the Senate about the marriage of women and the matrimonial law which will be productive of new offspring'. The verse is almost as flat in the original as in my prose translation; one can see why poets preferred to evade such unambiguous pronouncements. But Virgil does, in his own more indirect and allusive manner, show sympathy in the *Georgics* with the aims, if not with the methods, of Octavian. Nonetheless, it will also be argued in Chapter 3 that important elements in the *Georgics*, most notably the conclusion, suggest attitudes and emotions very different from straightforward moralising and unreflective patriotism. The construction of the poem is polyphonal; some of the voices convey a philosophical cosmopolitanism, others a sensuous melancholy. The idea of Rome is presented with a complexity which includes ambiguity.

Virgil also professes himself anxious to write an epic poem in glorification of Octavian's martial achievements. This was an object even dearer to Octavian's heart than support for his moral programme. The heir of Julius Caesar had by definition to be a great soldier; the ruler of Rome must embody the conquering glory of his people. Roman grandees, like Greek dynasts before them, had for a century-and-a-half been accustomed to receiving laudatory epics about their conquests. Cicero tried to induce quite a number of poets, Greek and Roman, to write an epic about his deeds in his consulship; in the end he was reduced to writing the poem himself, to the cruel mirth of the public. Virgil certainly encouraged Octavian to believe that he would 'soon' turn his mind to the production of such a poem (*G* 3.46ff.). In the end, however, he decided to write something very different – the *Aeneid*. We shall discuss his reasons in Chapter 4.

An epic poem in twelve books challenged Homer, but it also made towards him an immediate gesture of submission. For each of the two Homeric epics had twenty-four books and Virgil's total of twelve must have been meant to suggest a certain modesty – the *Aeneid* is only half of the *Iliad* or the *Odyssey*. Yet at the same time the *Aeneid* aspires to comprehend both Homeric epics: Odyssean wanderings in the first half, Iliadic battles in the second. Homer – 'the poet' as he is so often called in Greek – was the supreme figure of ancient literature, his genius universally recognised. Virgil rose to an extraordinary height of audacity in challenging comparison with him, and he was well aware of it. We are told that when criticised for his borrowings from Homer, he replied: 'Let them try it; they'll soon see that it is easier to take away Hercules' club than to take a single line from Homer.' And he had, as we shall see, set himself the task of absorbing and re-creating the whole of the Homeric epic.

In retrospect Virgil's career can be seen to assume a coherent shape, a crescendo of scale and subject. First came the comparatively modest model of a Hellenistic master, a small-scale poet with much to teach in euphony, harmony, and suggestiveness. In the *Eclogues* he took his first steps in blending Greek and Italian, imaginary and real, timeless and contemporary. Then he tackled an archaic poet who worked on a larger scale: his 'Ascraean' poem on the Italian countryside proved hospitable to deeply felt emotions and thoughts on the destiny of man and the fate of Rome. At last he was ready for the poem on a massive scale – twelve books and nearly 10,000 lines – in the grandest manner known to ancient poetry. It is tempting to think of the image of an aspiring fighter who works his way up through lesser but taxing opponents until he is ready to get into the ring with the champion.

Virgil worked on his epic for ten years. When he died in 19 BC it was not finished. It contains a number of lines which are metrically incomplete. Ancient taste did not share the Romantic liking for the fragmentary and the suggestive but expected works of art to be as perfect as possible. That the *Aeneid* was published and admired despite being visibly unfinished is a remarkable tribute to the impression it made on contemporaries. It seems that Virgil was not communicative about its contents. Propertius, writing about 25 BC, salutes the coming epic in hyperbolic terms but thinks of it as a poem about Octavian and the battle of Actium (ii.34.61). We hear on reliable authority that Augustus himself was kept in the dark: while he was away on campaign in Spain 'he sent letters in pleading vein and even in a tone of humorous menace, asking to be sent "even the first outline of the *Aeneid* or any section of it" '. The poet wrote in reply, 'I would send you anything which was worthy of your attention but I have taken on something so vast that I almost feel I must have been mad to start on it'.

The *Aeneid* was not by any means simply an attempt to write an old-style heroic epic, difficult as that would itself have been for a sensitive poet of Virgil's date. He had decided, for reasons to be more fully explained later, that it was not now possible to write an encomiastic epic about a contemporary without falling both into excessive adulation and also into absurd bathos. An heroic epic had to be set in the heroic period, the age of the myths; but the intention of writing a poem on Augustus was not abandoned when he set the epic in the distant past, a thousand years earlier, in the generation of the Trojan War. On the contrary, the mythological epic was also to be an epic about Augustus, who was to be brought into the poem both by explicit passages of prophecy and also by implicit means – by comparisons and juxtapositions which would suggest to the audience that the actions and sufferings of Aeneas alluded to those of the great leader who now presided over their destinies.

The story of Aeneas must in addition be paradigmatic not only of Augustus but also of the destiny of Rome in the most general terms – the glory and also the unhappiness of being an imperialist. The poem must conform to the very highest standards of technical refinement as displayed in *Eclogues* and *Georgics*. The formulaic repetitions and occasional lapses to which Homer was entitled by his antiquity were not possible nowadays for a poet with an artistic conscience. Virgil was a passionate reader, not only of Homer but also of many other poets, Greek and Roman. Attic tragedy, the refined Greek poets of the Alexandrian era, the classics of earlier Latin verse – all of them were to be laid under contribution. He was a student of mythology and history, too, who was aware that there were many discrepant and often contradictory versions of the stories he must use; he wanted to give hints and allusions to such versions in the course of his poem. The local antiquities of Italy must be brought in and somehow made to fit with the classic mythology of Greece. His studies of philosophy were profound and the *Aeneid* is pervaded by hints and echoes of them. There are passages which recall Plato, others of which the ancient commentators remark 'this is Stoic doctrine' or 'this is Epicurean'. All these were notes absent, of course, from Homer.

Above all Virgil was concerned to add two things, without which his evident determination that his poem should be all-inclusive and should omit nothing, would fail at the heart. First, he must do justice to a passionate Roman patriotism, without which Roman history became unintelligible and his epic would be pointless; here he found that the *Iliad*, by contrast, observes a serene and dispassionate objectivity between Greeks and Trojans. Second, he was hardly less anxious to do justice to an opposite set of feelings – those of regret and dismay at the human cost of empire. The career of conquest and dominion was not to be presented as enjoyable or as making the imperialist happy; the sacrifices so sternly demanded from Aeneas stand for the self-abnegation involved in turning away from the arts, from philosophy, and from ordinary life, to the exacting service of destiny.

While Virgil worked on the *Aeneid*, the victorious Octavian determined to show himself a benevolent and rational ruler. After the battle of Actium he had ostentatiously destroyed unread the compromising letters from Roman senators to Antony which fell into his hands. There was no proscription and no bloody settling of scores in Rome. His assumption of the name Augustus in 27 BC marked a break with the past, if not the assumption of a new identity – as when a Christian takes a new name at confirmation, or a Pope on election. 'Augustus' was a name unlike that of any Roman in history: the adjective means something like 'venerable' but with overtones less comfortable and more superhuman than those of an Anglican archdeacon. Octavian's violent past, stained by acts of bloodshed, proscriptions and expropriations, was thus put behind him. The world was organised and a façade of constitutionalism was preserved; but the realities of power were not difficult to see and those realities were that military force was now a monopoly of the new ruler. An aristocratic republic gave place to an autocracy in which aristocrats were allowed to hold great offices and to enjoy wealth and splendour, but not to make serious trouble. Although he was such an innovator, or because he was, Augustus made a show of conservatism. He claimed to follow ancient precedents, revived or invented ancient rituals, disclaimed untraditional honours. That cast of mind naturally fitted well with the antiquarian aspects of the *Aeneid*.

The *Eclogues* were written in a lawless period, the *Georgics* in the uneasy peace between civil wars, the *Aeneid* in a time in which one man, who had raised a private army and marched on Rome in his nineteenth year, and whose whole career had been essentially unconstitutional, was establishing himself as the permanent ruler of the Roman Empire. Augustus was intelligent and subtle; he offered himself as the deliverer of a world which, without him, would have crashed into final ruin. There was naturally a desire not only to accept his unavoidable power but also to believe in his benevolence and wisdom. It was also natural that his violent beginnings were never forgotten, as men reflected that at any time he could, if he chose, unleash again the horrors which he now professed to have renounced. In all three works of Virgil we shall find the theme of political power and armed force in their relation to the life of the intellect and the emotions, of philosophy, the arts and love. The poet's thought did not remain unchanging but in none of the poems is that relationship an easy or a happy one. It is his keen perception of this which, perhaps more than anything else, qualified Virgil to be the supreme poet of the imperial people of Rome.

Chapter 2

The *Eclogues*:
Rome and Arcadia

As we have seen, Virgil was at work on his book of pastoral
poems in the years 43-38 BC. Theocritus had set his herds-
men in Sicily, and they refer freely to Sicilian place names;
Virgil acknowledges that when he refers to his own 'Sicilian
Muse' and 'Syracusan verse'. But he has complicated this
simple matter in a most suggestive way. In the First *Eclogue*
the herdsmen, it soon emerges, live in the countryside near
a small town, from which one can make the journey to
Rome; in the Ninth they are at home near Mantua. More
confusingly, in the Seventh the singing contest takes place
on the Mincius, the river which flows by Mantua (7.13) and
yet the singers are 'both Arcadians' (7.4) – Greeks, that is,
from the land-locked middle of the Peloponnese. The char-
acters can talk of seeing their reflection in the sea (2.25) or
of committing suicide by leaping down into it (8.58-60), yet
neither Arcadia nor Mantua is anywhere near the sea-coast.
Several of the poems refer to hills and to the long shadows
which they cast at evening, yet the country round Mantua
is absolutely flat.

It seems that Arcadia, for Virgil, is not really a place which
can be found on a map; rather, it is an ideal, the home of
song and love. So in the Tenth *Eclogue* the lovelorn Gallus,
a real man and a friend of Virgil, wishes he had been born
an Arcadian:

Tristis at ille 'tamen cantabitis, Arcades', inquit,
'montibus haec vestris, soli cantare periti
Arcades. o mihi tum quam molliter ossa quiescant,
vestra meos olim si fistula dicat amores!
atque utinam ex vobis unus vestrique fuissem
aut custos gregis aut maturae vinitor uvae...'

                                              (10.31-6)

But sadly he replied, 'At least, you Arcadians, you will sing
to your hills of my suffering, you Arcadians who alone know
how to sing. O what soft repose my bones would find, if one
day your pipes should tell of my unhappy love! Would that
I had been one of you, a herdsman of your flocks or at work
on your ripe grapes...'

The invention and naming of Arcadia is Virgil's achieve-
ment, looking forward not only to the pastoral poetry of
Europe but to Handel's *Acis and Galatea* and to the paint-
ings of Claude (the most Virgilian of all artists) and of
Watteau. But there is something else – the desire to present
in the *Eclogues* a world which cannot be pinned down, one
harmonious whole which is not quite in Sicily, or in North
Italy, or in Greece. Theocritus' sharp eye for real places is
succeeded by a conscious desire to blur the outlines.

That point is worth making at the outset, because it is
true in other ways as well. The First *Eclogue*, which was the
first thing to be read by Virgil's contemporaries who picked
up the new book by a little-known young poet, presents
some teasing problems. It opens with a beautifully melodi-
ous speech:

Tityre, tu patulae recubans sub tegmine fagi
silvestrem tenui musam meditaris avena;
nos patriae finis et dulcia linquimus arva.
nos patriam fugimus; tu, Tityre, lentus in umbra
formosam resonare doces Amaryllida silvas.

                                              (1.1-5)

> You, Tityrus, are practising rustic music on your Pan-pipe,
> stretched out beneath a spreading beech; I am leaving my
> country and the fields I love. I am in flight from my country,
> while you, Tityrus, at ease in the shade, are making the
> woods resound to your love for Amaryllis.

Here are all the pastoral ingredients, the delightful spot in
the shade (this is a Mediterranean country), the music, love.
But another note is also sounded. Why is Meliboeus, the
first speaker, being driven into exile? Because, it soon
emerges, this Arcadia is near Rome and Roman politics are
invading the pastoral world where they do not belong.
'Godless soldiers' are to enjoy Meliboeus' land and the
harvest of his work: 'Look what misery civil war has pro-
duced – it was for them that we sowed our fields!' (1.71-2).
No reader can have been in any doubt that we have here
a scene from the evictions, when in 42 and 41 BC, after the
defeat of Brutus and Cassius, Mark Antony and Octavian
rewarded their victorious legions by confiscating and dis-
tributing land.

As for Tityrus, he tells us how he sought exemption for
himself. He went to Rome: 'The city men call Rome I used
in my ignorance to think of as like our local market town. I
simply compared small to large, as puppies resemble dogs
and kids resemble goats' (1.19-23). However, Rome, the
rustic discovers, is something of a quite different order. On
the first page of Virgil's work, amid the harmonious verse,
the discord makes itself heard, the impact of imperial power
on innocent happiness. The story of Tityrus' trip to Rome
is told in a confusing way. He went in quest of his freedom,
he tells us, having saved up the money to purchase it. 'Lucky
old man,' Meliboeus replies (1.46). That seems to mean that
he is an old slave, gone to buy his freedom from his master.
But this story is confused with another: Tityrus goes, not to
his own master, but to a 'divine young man', whom he

promises to worship like a god, who says: 'Pasture your cattle as before, boys.' (1.45). This suggests a freeholder rather than a slave; for slaves could not hold land. He has secured possession of his land without change ('as before'). There is, however, still the suggestion that he is a slave seeking the greatest change – his freedom, which only his owner could give him. Yet this unnamed young man 'was the first to' give a favourable response. Again Tityrus is an old man but the reply is to 'boys'.

Ever since antiquity readers have had trouble with this opening passage. The usual course has been to say that Tityrus 'is' (or 'stands for') Virgil himself and that the poem expresses his thanks to Octavian, who was conspicuously young to be in a position of power, for exempting him from the evictions. If so, he has taken some trouble to confuse the picture: we are left with the awkward fact that, after all, Meliboeus is turned out; and that it is his bitter lamentations which fill the second half of the poem. Can that really have been Virgil's idea of the way to say 'thank you'? The favour conferred on Tityrus is shown as purely arbitrary; for Meliboeus, equally innocent, there is no miraculous deliverer. The problem is compounded by the reappearance of the confiscations in the Ninth *Eclogue*. Here we find a character who resembles Virgil much more than the elderly slave Tityrus did. Menalcas lives near Mantua; he is a singer and a translator of Theocritus (we are given some snatches of his work). He had hoped to preserve his property by his song. Not only did he fail but was lucky to escape with his life (9.11ff.). It is not possible to make one story out of these two poems and we must accept that Virgil was not primarily interested in giving us an account of his own experience. These are scenes from the evictions – the sort of thing that is going on; and it is tragic. The poems exploit the discontinuity between contemporary Italian events and the distant world of Greek pastoral, in order to avoid being specific, to convey neither statistics of the ejections nor autobiography of the poet but, rather, the atmosphere and the emotional significance of events. Of course the temptation to inquire into the poet's own life is strong. I guess that what happened to him was that he was ejected and that his powerful friends then compensated him with property in a different part of Italy – the Bay of Naples. It is there, not in Mantua, that we find him living later. This series of transactions, if rightly inferred, was in any case inherently unpoetical; and it may have helped to move the poet towards a kind of writing which enabled him to express both gratitude and bitterness at the same time. That complexity of style was a lesson which was to show its importance above all in the *Aeneid*.

The *Eclogues* are ten separate poems but they are also carefully arranged into an elegant whole. At the end of the Fifth poem one of the two characters presents the other with a Pan-pipe, on which, he says: 'I played "Corydon was once on fire with love for Alexis" and "Whose flocks are these? Do they belong to Meliboeus?"' (5.84f.). That is to say, he quotes the opening lines of the Second and Third *Eclogues*. Thus there is a moment of pause and retrospection at the centre of the book. The Sixth poem opens with a fresh account of the poet's inspiration by Apollo. Evidently the central division is meant to be felt. The poems alternate in form, the odd-numbered ones being in dialogue and capable of performance by two or three speakers, while the even-numbered poems are narratives for a single speaker. The two longest *Eclogues* are the Third and Eighth, which come in the middle of the two halves of the book, and each contains eight lines in praise of Pollio, Virgil's patron. The three poems which depart furthest from the ordinary pastoral style are numbers 4, 5 and 6, placed together in the centre; and the two poems in which Virgil's friend the poet Gallus plays a role are 6 and 10, framing the second half of the collection. There are other patterns and connections which may be discovered by the reflective reader. The architecture of the *Eclogues* book seems to have made a considerable impression; and it is not by chance that so many of the books of the other Augustans contain ten poems or multiples of ten, that Horace, in particular, exhibits similar patterns in some of his collections. The *Georgics* and the *Aeneid* were to contain further evidence of Virgil's architectonic power.

The First *Eclogue* combines the idyllic with elements alien to Theocritus, giving the whole a more complex and problematic atmosphere. Virgil follows it in the Second with something rather simpler: an unhappy lover sits and bewails his plight to the rustic scenery. Theocritean models are clear. But here too something has changed; for Virgil replaces the pretty girls who rebuff their suitors (in Theocritus' Third and Eleventh *Idylls*) with a homosexual passion, that of Corydon for the boy Alexis who is the favourite of his master. Corydon is in the country, the boy apparently in the town; even beyond that, the social situation of the two, in any case, means that this love is absolutely without hope. The elegance of the poem lies in the depiction of poor Corydon's train of thought as he spends the whole day mooning over his love. He begins by reproaching the distant Alexis for disregarding his song, reflects that it would have been better to fall in love with somebody else (he names another boy and also a girl – this is a bewildered singer), protests that after all he is not so ineligible or unattractive, and imagines the delights of life together in the country. This passage of delicious fantasy, the centre of the poem, gives place to the provocative threat that he will bestow on a girl the pastoral presents, a Pan-pipe and two baby goats, which he is keeping for Alexis. Then a last ecstatic appeal ('Come to me, o lovely boy!') is followed by a collapse into despair ('You are rustic indeed, Corydon; Alexis does not care for your presents and, if you were competing in presents, Iollas [the master] would not admit defeat.' [2.56f.]). Corydon ends by conceding that his hopeless passion, natural though it is, is ruining his life; he has work to do, which he is neglecting. Another Alexis will be kinder, if this one will not. That apparently strong-minded conclusion has been under-cut in advance by the opening of the poem, where we read that he came 'day after day' and sang this monologue among the trees. Poor Corydon, we see, will be back tomorrow. We are to appreciate the delicate art which makes the singer at once sympathetic and absurd, with his rustic treasures and his high-flown touches ('Why fly from me? Gods have lived in the woods and so did Paris of Troy' [2.60f.]) arguments hardly likely to weigh with a pampered slave-boy, even if he were there to listen to them. This poem represents the furthest extreme in the *Eclogues* from real life, yet even here we may suspect a hidden element of reality. The pretty girls of Theocritus are replaced by a pretty boy. The scandal which ancient gossip had to tell about Virgil was of a homosexual sort and the sensibility of the *Aeneid*, as we shall see, does not, to say the least, contradict that implication.

Two of the *Eclogues* represent singing competitions, in which two singers take it in turns to cap verses. In the Third the unit is two lines, in the Seventh it is four. We find the regular furniture of pastoral, as, for instance, in the following exchange:

> – The junipers and the prickly chestnuts are motionless; under every tree all round us lies the fruit. Now all things smile, but if the lovely Alexis were to leave our hills you would see even the rivers run dry.
> – The fields are dry, the grass is dying of thirst and the tainted air; the wine god grudges the hills the shadow of the vine. When our Phyllis comes every bush will be green, and Jupiter will come down in showers of refreshing rain.

> (7.53-60)

Such verses as these, where pure prettiness is supreme, inspired Alexander Pope in his early Pastorals – for instance:

— All Nature mourns, the skies relent in showers,
  Hush'd are the birds, and closed the drooping flowers;
  If Delia smile, the flowers begin to spring,
  The skies to brighten, and the birds to sing.
— All Nature laughs, the groves are fresh and fair,
  The sun's mild lustre warms the vital air;
  If Sylvia smiles, new glories gild the shore,
  And vanquished nature seems to smile no more.

                                    (*The First Pastoral*, 69-76)

Virgil was not content to stay on this level, however. In the Fourth *Eclogue* he begins by calling on his Sicilian Muses for 'a slightly grander song', to greet the consulship of his patron Pollio. Although pastoral touches continue to characterise the poem, more exalted and ambitious notes mingle with them: 'The last age of the Sibyl's prophecy has come, the great cycle of ages born anew. Now the Virgin returns, the Age of Saturn returns and a new race comes down from the skies.... Do you, goddess of childbirth, look kindly on the child whose birth will end the iron race and bring in the golden all over the world' (4.4-9). The Virgin is the goddess of justice, who left the earth long ago in horror at the wickedness of men. The identity of the child who is to be born has been disputed from Virgil's own lifetime. He is sprung from gods; his cradle shall put forth flowers and in his childhood the serpent shall die out and flocks shall have no fear of lions. In his maturity the whole earth shall bear every crop without cultivation; agriculture and trade will both be things of the past. The world shakes in joyous expectation of the new age: 'Begin, little child, to smile in greeting to your mother –your mother has borne ten [lunar] months of discomfort. Begin, little child...' (4.60-2).

The poem was for a thousand years accepted as a prophecy of the birth of Christ, for obvious reasons – the Virgin, the child and the resemblance to the Messianic prophecies of Isaiah ('the wolf shall dwell with the lamb, and the leopard shall lie down with the kid, and the calf and the young lion together; and a little child shall lead them'). Nowadays that may seem naïve but we should not rush to the opposite extreme and reduce the poem, as some scholars now do, into a purely human and occasional one. Pollio was consul in the year 40 BC and his poet should have had this poem ready on the day when he assumed office, 1 January. At that time the political horizon was extremely dark. After the horrors of the last three years it seemed that Antony and Octavian were about to come to blows in another round of civil war. In the event things were patched up in the autumn of 40, the two dynasts making an agreement (the 'pact of Brundisium'), which was strengthened by Antony marrying Octavian's sister, the excellent Octavia. Most scholars, it seems take the Fourth *Eclogue* to be a celebration of that union and the child to be the son expected from it. But the language is altogether too hyperbolic for such a political marriage, whose issue was, in fact, to be two daughters and then the husband deserting Octavia for Cleopatra. The language is indeed prophetic and the Messianic parallels are real; for by this date Jewish literature was available in Greek and other Eastern peoples – Egyptians and Babylonians – were also producing apocalyptic writings which became known in the West. The Fourth *Eclogue* is more plausibly to be understood, not as a response to a political settlement which seemed to ensure peace but, on the contrary, as the work of a mind which, in despair at the situation on earth, takes refuge in hopes and fantasies of another order. Those are the circumstances in which Messianic literature is normally produced and Virgil used all sorts of material – a poem of Catullus, Greek myth, prophetic books, pastoral – to produce his haunting poem.

In the Fifth *Eclogue* Virgil presents two herdsmen who sing, this time not in rivalry but in succession, of the cruel death and the deification of Daphnis. That is the name of

a doomed youth in Theocritus' First poem, who wastes away
for love of a nymph. Virgil, however, has removed the erotic
motif. At Daphnis' death all nature mourned; but now he
is a god, benevolent and a bringer of peace to the country-
side, in return for their eager worship. Who is Daphnis? Ever
since antiquity it has been felt that there are hints of the
assassination of Julius Caesar. That tremendous event was
in the very recent past, the utterly unexpected killing of the
man who held the supreme power in the world. In the
convulsions which followed men saw terrifying portents,
above all the comet which appeared on the day of his
funeral and which was immediately declared by Octavian
to be Caesar's soul. Virgil will write of those portents, the
marks of divine anger with the world, at the end of the First
Georgic – darkness at midday, an eruption of Mount Etna,
the appearance of ghosts and the hearing of supernatural
voices. Caesar was forthwith declared to be a god and
Octavian, his grandnephew and adopted son, officially
called himself 'son of a god' (*divi filius*). Readers of the Fifth
Eclogue cannot have failed to recall these things.

Despite this Daphnis is carefully made unlike Caesar –
not a general and ruler, middle-aged and bald, but a young
and beautiful herdsman (yet 'shepherd of the people' is a
phrase for a ruler familiar ever since Homer, and doubtless
the new god is rejuvenated); not a notorious sceptic in
religion but a pious devotee of Bacchus, yet Caesar was
pontifex maximus, the official head of Roman religion. The
technique is one of suggesting yet denying identity: through
the figure of Daphnis the Roman reader was meant to detect
some glimmer of the figure of Caesar. This technique be-
comes important in the *Aeneid*, where Aeneas allows us to
catch glimpses of Augustus, while Dido, the African queen
seducing the Roman from his duty, at moments evokes
Cleopatra.

The Sixth and Tenth *Eclogues* honour Virgil's friend

Cornelius Gallus. This man was a phenomenon: from inconspicuous origins in Gaul he had risen to celebrity both as a man of action and as a poet. He was regarded as the inventor of the Latin love elegy, represented for us by a simple papyrus, discovered in 1978, giving some nine lines and by the works of his successors – Tibullus, Propertius, and Ovid. He also served Octavian so effectively that, after the defeat of Antony and Cleopatra in 31 BC, he was appointed first Roman viceroy of Egypt. In that lofty position he came to grief; for reports reached Rome that he was showing signs of grasping glory for himself instead of reserving it all for his master. He was disgraced and in despair took his own life (26 BC). The Sixth *Eclogue* is a puzzling poem. It opens with a passage in which the poet says he was about to write martial epic but Apollo pinched his ear and told him that, while a shepherd should fatten up his sheep, he should keep his poems slender (6.4f.). This instruction echoes a celebrated poem of Callimachus (a Greek poet contemporary with Theocritus), a combative and polemical writer with an aesthetic which demanded in poetry small-scale and exquisite technique, not loosely written and conventional epics. That the author of this *Eclogue* should have gone on to write the *Aeneid* must count as one of the surprises of literary history. That the author of the *Aeneid* should in youth have expressed this Callimachean view shows how many were the difficulties which he had to overcome to write his great mythological poem.

The Sixth *Eclogue* continues in a way which shows the attraction for Virgil of a certain self-conscious, almost decadent, kind of poetry. He tells of the drunken Silenus, a minor deity in the retinue of Bacchus, singing a song which begins with the creation of the world out of atoms swirling through the void – an echo, in content and in form, of the great poem of Lucretius, *On the Nature of the Universe*. Then, once the forests and seas have appeared in the world, the song goes on to tell stories from mythology – Prometheus chained to the rock, the loss by Hercules of his beloved boy Hylas, and the tale of Pasiphae and the bull. Four lines take us from the first appearance of mankind to Pasiphae, no less than sixteen being lavished on a plangent account of her perverse passion:

a, virgo infelix, quae te dementia cepit?

(6.47)

Alas, poor maid, what madness has enthralled you?

And a little later (6.52):

Alas, poor maid, you are straying over the hills, but his snow-white flank reposes on a soft bed of flowers, and under a dark ilex tree he chews the sallow cud; or he pursues some female in the great herd. 'Close the ways through the woods, you Nymphs: close them, you Nymphs of Dicté; perhaps the bull's wandering tracks will meet our eyes'.

Both the length and the sympathetic tone of all this are most remarkable. The passion of Pasiphae, enamoured of the bull and the mother of the Minotaur, was generally regarded as a monstrous aberration, to be explained only as a punishment from the gods. There seems no evident reason why this bizarre tale should loom so large. Virgil appears to be showing here the sensibility which might have made him a minor poet, an author of perversely pretty works like the *Zmyrna* of Cinna (the story of a girl who fell in love with her father) or the *Ciris* in the *Virgilian Appendix* (the story, by contrast, of a girl who betrayed her father and her country because of her passion for an enemy). At the end of this particular path stands Oscar Wilde's *Salome*. Virgil resisted the temptation and made himself into a major poet; but glimpses of that sensibility will recur. Pasiphae herself makes two appearances in the *Aeneid* (6.24ff., 6.447); and again there is no hint of censure in either passage.

Then another unexpected transition introduces Gallus – how he met the Muses on Mount Helicon, was complimented by them and given a pipe which once belonged to Hesiod. Mount Helicon is in Northern Greece and it would be naïve to imagine that in reality Gallus had ever set foot there. This is an allegorical scene: Gallus will be the successor of Hesiod – a role which would in fact be played by Virgil himself in the *Georgics*. The *Eclogues* end (Tenth) with Gallus again and again he is in scenery of symbolic significance. This time it is Arcadia, the place newly defined by Virgil as an ideal home of love and song. Gallus' great poetic achievement was his elegies on his tormented love for the fair but cruel Lycoris, a poetical cover-name for a real woman, a high-class *demi-mondaine* named Cytheris, whose spectacular career had included liaisons with both Mark Antony and Brutus. One celebrated poem, imitated by Propertius, portrayed the poet lamenting his desertion by Lycoris, who has gone off with another man –not, one feels, an event which can have surprised Gallus much in real life. He loves her too much to reproach her and, in an ecstasy of masochism, hopes that, as she goes off over the mountains, she will not cut her feet on the ice.

Virgil transposes this from Gallus' metre, elegiac couplets, into his own bucolic hexameters. He presents Gallus in the role of Daphnis in Theocritus' First poem, dying for love, surrounded by the sympathy of the shepherds and the rustic gods. As an Arcadian rustic, of course, Gallus does not write and publish poems. He sings and hopes that the people of Arcady will sing his songs when he is dead of love; and he writes his love in the bark of trees. This rustic echoes Gallus' own lamentation:

> tu procul a patria (nec sit mihi credere tantum)
> Alpinas a! dura, nives et frigora Rheni
> me sine sola vides. a, te ne frigora laedant!
> a, tibi ne teneras glacies secet aspera plantas!   (10.46-9)

> You are far from home (if only I could disbelieve such a
> thing), looking on the snowy Alps and frozen Rhine: O cruel!
> alone, without me. O, may the frosts not hurt you! O, may
> the rough ice not cut your soft feet!

Greeks and Romans constantly speak of poetry in terms which for us belong only to music: poets 'sing'; the pastoral poet plays on the Pan-pipes; the rhythms of verse are intimately connected with dancing. Here is an example of another way in which music can help us to understand how a classical poet works. What Virgil has produced in the Tenth *Eclogue* is something which in music would not surprise us at all but which seems strange in poetry. He has written a variation, in his own style, on a theme by Gallus, transposing the elegiac lover – a man about town in love with a known, even notorious, woman of Rome – into a pastoral figure by Virgil out of Theocritus, enduring and vocalising his amorous pain in Arcadia. The musical change involved in turning elegiac couplets into hexameters is part of the pleasure of the work, which is, of course, among other things, a tremendous compliment to his friend.

Virgil ends the *Eclogues* with a coda of eight lines (70ff.). That is enough of pastoral song: the shades of evening are failing, it is time to drive home the flocks after a day of bucolic singing. The understated conclusion rounds off the collection with a dying fall, like that of Milton's *Lycidas*:

> So sang the uncouth Swain to th' Oaks and rills,
> While the still morn went out with Sandals gray...
> And now the Sun had stretch't out all the hills,
> And now was dropt into the Western bay;
> At last he rose, and twitch't his Mantle blue:
> Tomorrow to fresh Woods, and Pastures new.

In both poems the setting of the sun provides a natural and harmonious end to what is imagined as the song of a shepherd, sitting by his flock until it is time to drive it home. That elegance does not entirely conceal a certain grave irony. For the author of *Lycidas* could not be taken for an uncouth swain; and the singer of the *Eclogues*, too, has shown how exquisitely he can combine simplicity and complexity. The *Eclogues* are a beautiful collection of poems, the most subtly melodious verse which the Latin language had yet known. They contain passages, like the soliloquy of Corydon and the passion of Pasiphae, which dally with a languorous unreality – hot-house fruit; others in which the poet has tried to deal, gingerly and in an oblique fashion, with contemporary happenings. The author of the *Eclogues* is young. At moments he has yielded to the temptation to show off his learning and his cleverness; not every change of gear is smooth and there are places, like Tityrus' story in the First *Eclogue*, where compression and combination lead to obscurity. It remained to be seen what further progress this promising poet could make.

Chapter 3

The *Georgics*:
the Muse in hobnails

In the thirties Virgil turned his mind to the creation of a poem on a larger scale – 2,000 lines divided into four books. His model, as we have seen, was the archaic Greek poet Hesiod and the *Georgics* took the form of a didactic poem on farming. That flat description gives very little idea of the *Georgics*; but it does give us a point from which to analyse the real nature of this beautiful but elusive poem – 'the best work of the best poet', as it was called by the greatest of Virgil's translators, John Dryden. In a similar way the poet gives us an apparently clear statement of the poem's motivation, calling it 'your hard instructions, Maecenas' (*G* 3.41); that, too, can hardly be taken literally.

Hesiod was a small farmer in Boeotia, in northern Greece. His two poems – the *Works and Days* (a better translation might be *Jobs and Calendar*) and the *Theogony* – are works in rather rough-and-ready hexameters which profess to give instruction to the audience (rather than the reader; for this is pre-literary verse). The *Theogony* explains the nature and history of the gods, how the world came into existence and how earlier high gods were in the end succeeded by Zeus. *Works and Days* is a sort of handbook for farmers, which also includes a strong moralising element, Hesiod has suffered injustice, he tells us, at the hands of an unscrupulous brother and corrupt local magnates (or 'kings')

and his poem combines practical instructions on agricul-
ture with harsh criticism of these men and the exposition of
the proper way of life. 'Work and pray' is a pervasive theme.
The farmer should observe justice and piety as he follows
the rhythm of hard work which accompanies the changing
seasons of the year. Hesiod has a sour sense of humour, a
strong vein of peasant misogyny, occasional moments which
rise to real poetry, and a perceptible difficulty in organising
his material and passing from one point or story to the next.
At times, indeed, he is reduced to such expedients as saying:
'Now, if you like, I'll tell you another story.'

Clearly Virgil, having shown the literary sophistication
and technical bravura of the *Eclogues*, could not really go on
to produce something like this. Hesiod was a venerable
figure of the distant past; it would be a very different thing
for a modern poet to emulate his quaintness of technique
and his simple attitudes. Another important point was that
didactic poetry itself had by now changed its function.
When Hesiod composed, there was no such thing as literary
prose and even the most unpoetical subject-matter, as later
taste would feel it to be, could find literary expression in
verse, the poetic form helping to make it memorable in the
minds of unlettered people. Some of the pre-Socratic phi-
losophers in the early fifth century BC still wrote in verse.
But the rise and triumph of prose, the great event in the
history of Greek literature, meant that after 400 BC it was
an eccentricity to try to set out in verse subject-matter which
could more clearly and more rationally be dealt with in that
medium. This was especially so, as the rise of prose went
hand in hand with a great increase in the body of know-
ledge, some of it highly technical, of the sort which a manual
of instruction might be expected to contain. Consequently
the 'second generation' of Greek didactic poets in the
Hellenistic era were very different from those of archaic
Greece. These men enjoyed the challenge of turning into

polished verse specialised works which already existed in prose. Thus Aratus of Soli (writing about 310 BC) versified prose treatises on the constellations and on weather signs. The poem in which he did this, the *Phaenomena*, had an extraordinary success: it was translated into Latin by Cicero, and Virgil makes use of it at several points in the First *Georgic*. Such works were, it may be felt, essentially frivolous, with no real reason for existing except the sophisticated pleasure of savouring the contrast between dry content and elegant verse.

It was Lucretius, the great and isolated Latin poet of the generation before Virgil, who put new and unexpected life into this withering form. His poem *On the Nature of the Universe* embodied a programme which might have seemed no less perverse and artificial than, say, the Greek poem of Nicander *On Poisonous Animals*. This was a versification of the doctrines of the philosopher Epicurus, including the atomic theory. However, Lucretius transformed the subject by bringing to his poem the passionate tones of a devotee: by a strange paradox Epicurus' ideal of tranquillity of mind is preached with fervour; even the driest parts of his system receive an emotional impetus very different from the dogmatic but dispassionate manner of the philosophers himself, whom Lucretius declares to have been a god. That strength of emotion in a didactic setting was a remarkable thing, quite alien to the ostentatious coolness of Hellenistic poems on such subjects. It gave Virgil a vital clue as he pondered the choice of theme for a poem of a larger scale and on a less remote topic than the *Eclogues*.

In the eighteenth century there were English gentlemen, educated in the classics, who thought they could actually use the *Georgics* as an adequate manual of instruction on agriculture. If one had a reliable land-agent, who filled in the gaps and used his own knowledge and common sense, one could indeed have the illusion that one was practising

Virgilian farming and no disaster need come of it. Virgil and Maecenas would, however, have been greatly surprised by such a procedure. Anyone who seriously wanted a farmer's manual could buy the work *On Agriculture* by Varro, the most learned of the Romans, which appeared in the mid-thirties and was used as a source by Virgil. Varro's treatise in three books contains masses of helpful detail, is organised on a rational and consistent plan and tells the reader what things cost, what profit margins can be expected, how large a work-force is needed for a farm of a given size. Varro also does not mind getting his hands dirty: he gives detailed instructions for the siting of the manure pit ('some people place the privies for the servants above it'); for the provision of muddy wallowing places for sows ('this is their form of refreshment, as bathing is for us'); and for ensuring that the lay-out of sheep-pens does not allow the animals' urine to stand in the stalls.

Varro's rather simple sense of humour is indulged by giving to the characters who speak in his work names which, while really in use among Romans, transparently relate to farm animals and the like – Fundanius (from *fundus*, a farm), Tremellius Scrofa (*scrofa* means 'sow'), Vaccius (*vacca* is a cow) and so on. It may be remarked in passing that the prevalence of such names at Rome is itself revealing: senators and grandees were still so close to the peasant style of their ancestors that names like 'Sow', 'Puppy' (*catulus*) and 'Blackbird' (*merula*) were common among them, in notable contrast with the practice of Greece, where names were given for dignity and prestige. Varro opens his treatise with a dedication, addressed to his wife, in which he says that he would have liked to have more time, so as to get his material into a better shape: 'But now I must set it out as best I can, reflecting that I need to hurry. They say man is a bubble, and an old man is all the more so. My eightieth year reminds me to gather up my luggage before I depart'.

The charming informality of all this was very different from the tone of anything which could possibly have been written by Virgil.

However, Virgil read the works of his chosen models with unrivalled penetration, as we shall see when we discuss his use of Homer in the *Aeneid*. In Varro's work, laxly written in point of style but full of material, he could find useful hints on subjects more ambitious than manure pits and sheep-pens. Varro includes some passages of a moral and patriotic character: he deplores the ostentation of the present as compared with the admirable simplicity of the past; he makes his speakers gather round a map of Italy and reflect on its superiority to less happy lands: 'What useful product is there which does not grow to perfection in Italy? What wheat shall I compare to that of Apulia, what wine to Falernian, what olive oil to that from Venafrum? Isn't it true that Italy is so covered with trees that the whole country is like an orchard?' (*On Agriculture* 1.2.6). By contrast, he ends his first book with a shocking scene of contemporary life in Rome. A servant rushes in, greatly distressed, with the news that the man for whom they were all waiting has just been stabbed to death in the street; he could not see who did it, but heard a voice in the crowd say that a mistake had been made. 'We went our separate ways', says Varro sadly, 'feeling distress at the human condition but no surprise that such a thing should happen at Rome.' These passages gave Virgil the hint for his magnificent praise of Italy (*G* 2.136ff.); and perhaps also for the emotional passage which ends his First book, on the horrors which punished Italy for the murder of Julius Caesar (*G* 1.466-514). Both are on a far larger scale and in a much more ambitious style than the brief touches in Varro.

Let us first consider the *Georgics* in their ostensible role of a didactic poem on agriculture. They do, indeed, contain instructions, sometimes whole strings of them, but direct injunctions add up to only a small proportion of the poem and many important agricultural operations are not described at all. For example, the Elder Cato, who wrote a book on agriculture in the first half of the second century BC – the earliest surviving work in Latin prose, as it happens – lists the equipment which is needed on a farm of given acreage. For a farm of 160 acres he lists more than ninety types of items including such things as 8 forks, 8 hoes, 4 spades, 5 shovels, 2 rakes, 8 scythes, 5 straw-hooks, 5 pruning-hooks, 3 axes, 3 wedges, etc. (*On Agriculture* Chap. 10). Virgil, by contrast, writes:

> We must describe the hardy countryman's weapons, without which the harvest cannot be planted and cannot grow: the ploughshare first and the heavy timbers of the curving plough, and the slow-rolling wagons of the Great Mother of Eleusis, threshers and drags, and the cruel weight of the harrow; then the cheap wickerwork equipment of Celeus, hurdles of arbutus wood and the mystic winnowing-fan of Iacchus. All these you will lay by providently beforehand.
>
> (*G* 1.160ff.)

We may observe several things about this passage. First, there are no indications of number or quantity. We have passed from the style of a competently written recipe book ('5 eggs, 2 ounces of flour') to that of a poetic evocation of a feast. Secondly, the range of equipment is dramatically reduced – not that Virgil wants his farmer to have fewer tools, rather because this is not a real catalogue but an artful shadow of one. And finally, there is the choice of images and of objects: the 'weapons' of the rustic; the 'cruel' weight of the harrow; the choice of those items of farm equipment which can be glorified by a connection with Greek myth and ritual. Cato, in his straightforward way, lists 'three large carts', whereas Virgil, since wagons were used in the famous Attic cult of Demeter, goddess of agriculture, feels free to speak of his farm waggons with the addition of this irrelevant but splendid association. Celeus and Iacchus are minor figures in the Eleusinian mystery cult, who dignify the other objects in this pseudo-catalogue, all too prosaic in themselves, with a related shimmer of religious and poetic interest.

That represents an extreme example of Virgil's anxiety about the stylistic level of his material and, consequently, of his poem. He expresses it once explicitly, in the Third book which concerns animals. There he deals at length with horses and cattle, large and impressive creatures, about which there were serious myths and for which there were serious events such as the chariot-race at the Olympic Games –undoubtedly poetical themes. The moment comes to pass to sheep and goats: 'This is the source from which lusty farmers must hope for glory'. Then:

> nec sum animi dubius verbis ea vincere magnum
> quam sit et angustis hunc addere rebus honorem;
> sed me Parnasi deserta per ardua dulcis
> raptat amor; iuvat ire iugis, qua nulla priorum
> Castaliam molli devertitur orbita clivo.
> nunc, veneranda Pales, magno nunc ore sonandum.

>   (*G* 3.289ff.)

> I am in no doubt how hard it is to prevail over this subject in words and to add distinction to so humble a theme; but over the unpeopled slopes of Parnassus I am whirled along by rapturous desire. It is a joy to go where no wheel of chariot before me has marked the soft grass, going down to the Castalian spring. Now, great goddess of the sheep-folds, now, if ever, I must speak in a fuller tone!

It is interesting to see the nature of Virgil's apprehension and the way he meets it. As soon as he has uttered the idea, he takes wing in a highly poetical little rhapsody, marked by the prominence of Greek place names which refer to the classic haunts of the Muses. The passage also deliber-ately recalls a striking passage of Lucretius (1.925ff.), who similarly claimed originality. It concludes with the injunction to himself to speak 'in a fuller tone' – to make up for his humble subject. And so he does, finding occasion for two spectacular set-pieces, one on the summer pasturing of the nomads of North Africa, the other on the opposite extreme – the snow-bound winters of the Scythians, drinking their beer underground. Neither of these, of course, is very obviously relevant to the experience of an Italian farmer except in so far as the poet contrives to suggest how diametrically opposed they are to the happy mean, to the temperate climate of Italy.

Virgil also has at his disposal less external means of converting his material into poetry. For instance, he takes a passage from Varro which does not seem extremely promising – an account of driving cattle to different pastures at different times of day:

> In summer time they begin feeding at daybreak, because at that time the grass is filled with dew and more agreeable than the drier grass of midday. At sunrise they are driven to water, to make them keener to graze when they come back again. In the midday heat, until it cools down, they are driven under shady rocks and spreading trees to cool off. In the evening air they graze again till sunset.
>
> (*On Agriculture* 2.2.10f.)

Here is what Virgil makes of that dry recital:

> When the sweet summer, welcomed in by the West Winds, sends sheep and goats too out into the glades and pastures, let us set out with the first glimpse of the Morning Star to the chilly fields, while the morning is fresh, while the turf is white, and while the dew on the soft grass is most delicious to the flocks. Then, when the fourth hour of sun creates a thirst and the bushes are buzzing with the shrill cry of the cicadas, I'll tell you to bring your flock to wells and to deep pools, to drink the water that runs in the wooden channels. But in the midday heat seek out a shady vale, if there is a

mighty oak, the tree of Jupiter, with aged trunk holding out
its massive branches, or a copse lies dark in the haunted
shade of many an ilex tree. Then give them the running water
again and pasture them again as the sun goes down, while
the cool Evening Star chills the air, the dewy moonlight
refreshes the glens, the kingfisher is heard on the river bank,
and the thickets re-echo to the goldfinch.   (G 3.322-38)

Comparison of the original (in which all the poetry is
invisible, like water underfoot in a dry landscape) with the
charming Virgilian orchestration shows the ability of the
poet to transform: the cicadas, the birds, the stars, the moon,
the emphasis on the emotional quality of everything –
sweet summer, delicious dew, the fully imagined trees and
plants. The merely practical atmosphere of rational action
in pursuit of profit is replaced by a vision of life full of natural
beauty and aesthetic pleasure.

There are many such passages. One might point, for
instance, to the rhapsodic description of the blessedness of
Italy (G 2.136ff.), including the lines which must haunt any
reader of the *Georgics* who travels in that country:

adde tot egregias urbes operumque laborem,
tot congesta manu praeruptis oppida saxis
fluminaque antiquos subterlabentia muros.   (G 2.155-7)

Consider also all our noble cities and the works of our hands,
all the towns piled up on sheer cliffs, and the rivers that glide
beneath ancient walls.

The mention of spring as the season for sowing leads the
poet into an eloquent account of the spring in all its effects
on nature. Moved by the thought, Virgil goes on:

Such, I am sure, are the days that shone when the world
began its growth, such was their radiant course: it was
spring; the great globe enjoyed the spring; they were spared
the blasts of the wintry East winds, when the first cattle
drank in the light and men, creatures of earth, first raised

their heads from the hard ground, when the forests were
filled with beasts and the sky was filled with stars.

(*G* 2.336ff.)

It does less than justice to Virgil to regard such passages as
simply purple patches of poetry superficially attached to the
grey texture of a manual of instruction. What he aims to do
is more than that – to present a picture of the farmer's life,
which is not only a moral example in all its simplicity and
severity, to the luxurious and demoralised city-dweller (that
note is also struck), but which also shows it as organically
related to the processes of nature, dignified and also beau-
tiful in its own right.

Hard work (*labor*) is important to this vision. Virgil evokes
the model of Hesiod in ascribing it to the will of the supreme
god. Hesiod gave a dark picture of the activities of Zeus,
who in his anger at being tricked by Prometheus, punished
mankind, both by the invention of the first woman (how the
race had got along before Pandora's arrival is not explained)
to torment men, and also by 'concealing livelihood'. Before
that happened, says Hesiod bitterly, 'One day's work would
have kept you for a year; you could soon hang up the rudder
of your boat on the wall; and there would be an end to the
labours of oxen and mules. But Zeus hid all this away'.
(*Works and Days* 42ff.). In fact, says Hesiod, 'The father of
gods and men laughed aloud' as he devised disaster for
mankind. That pungent and unedifying account is consid-
erably changed by Virgil. For him work is a positive value
and, in ordaining it as the human lot, Jupiter was certainly
not motivated by a malicious hostility:

The Father himself wished the path of cultivation not to be
an easy one. He was the first to make it an art to turn the
soil, sharpening our mortal wits with toil. He did not suffer
his realm to be lethargic and idle...he put venom into the
black serpents, made wolves into beasts of prey, knocked off
the honey from the leaves of trees...so that practice and

> thought should hammer out the various techniques (*ut*
> *varias usus meditando extunderet artis*).   (*G* 1.121-33)

So men are forced to acquire and practise the skills of hard labour and, by divine decree, anything which is not constantly worked on falls back and degenerates. Man is like a rower toiling to propel his boat upstream, who cannot stop without being carried backwards (*G* 1.199ff.). Yet there is a moral purpose underlying the need. In the First book the emphasis is more heavily on toil but with no shortage of indications that there could be an optimistic view of human life. In the Second that optimistic view is predominant. The farmer's work comes round in a cycle (*G* 2.401f.) and the year treads in its own footsteps; but the vine-dresser, for all his toil, sings as he finishes his rows. The olive tree needs no tending to produce the rich olive beloved of Peace; the apple-tree reaches up towards the stars with no need of our help; every copse is heavy with fruit and the bird-land, untilled, is scarlet with blood-red berries. 'And do men hang back from sowing and taking trouble?' (*G* 2.401-33). Such a passage shows Virgil's power, passing from a plain statement of fact – every year brings the same round of tasks – through a crescendo of vividly imagined and emotionally rendered detail to a final triumphant outburst. When nature has done so much, can man really be in two minds about playing his part? He goes on here to a richly elaborated list of trees and timber and is led back into a second and much fuller development of the idea of cooperation with nature:

> O fortunatos nimium, sua si bona norint,
> agricolas! quibus ipsa procul discordibus armis
> fundit humo facilem victum iustissima tellus.
>
> (*G* 2.458-60)

> O all too lucky countrymen, if only they knew their good fortune! Far from the clash of weapons of war the most righteous earth pours forth for them an easy livelihood.

As much as to say that, if man does his bit, the earth will respond in overflowing measure.

Romans always felt a certain guilt at having turned away from the robust and simple rustic life of their ancestors to a luxurious and cosmopolitan city existence. That feeling was of course accompanied by another, very different, one – pride and satisfaction at a career of unbroken conquest, which must mean that the gods favoured Rome and had glorified her with the splendours of the world. Virgil articulates both ideas, which were not capable of completely harmonious resolution, with memorable richness. The innocent life of the rustic, blessed and in harmony with nature, is the life which produces the ancient virtues: 'Young men hardened to labour and used to living on little, old men worthy of respect, and veneration for the gods' (*G* 2.472-3). Among such people is the last haunt of justice on earth. As for the poet, he tells us that his ambition would be to understand the secrets of nature, the causes of earthquake and eclipse:

> Happy is he who has power to know the causes of things and trample underfoot the fear of death! But lucky too is he who knows the rustic deities, Pan, Silvanus, and the nymphs. He is unmoved by the insignia of rank, by the crimson robe of kings or by the civil war which breaks faith between brothers; he is unmoved by the march of the scheming Dacian from the Danube, by the Roman Empire and power which must pass away.   (*G* 2.490-8)

This passage contains a tribute to Lucretius, the great predecessor in emotional didactic verse, but also a claim for the very different values of Virgil. Lucretius dismissed Pan and the nymphs as childish fantasies; Virgil loves and cherishes such deities. His mind is attached to the quiet values of the country life.

So deeply, in fact, is he attached to them that he feels supreme indifference towards the life of politics and of power, even towards Rome herself. What does it matter if barbarian hordes are massing on the frontiers? Even the rule of Rome must in the end pass away and, in the timeless perspective of the countryman, secure in his simple virtues and his timeless existence, that is a matter of indifference. As William Blake puts it:

> The sword sung on the barren heath,
> The sickle in the fruitful field:
> The sword he sung a song of death,
> But could not make the sickle yield.

The countryman, Virgil continues, is free from many forms of crime and folly. Not for him the horrors of civil war, the madness of political competition, the lust for opulence which drives men into avarice and wickedness. All this seems to be the expression of an essentially simple set of values, surprising indeed in the poet who was so shortly to embark on the supreme epic of Rome, but comprehensible in terms of one paticular line of ancient thought. However, Virgil pursues that line in an unexpected direction. The simple peasant life, upright and robust, free from luxury and from vice, is that of the good old peoples of Italy:

> hanc olim veteres vitam coluere Sabini,
> hanc Remus et frater; sic fortis Etruria crevit
> scilicet et rerum facta est pulcherrima Roma,
> septemque una sibi muro circumdedit arces.
>
> (*G* 2.532-5)

> This was the life of the Sabine people of old, this was the life of Romulus and Remus. Thus it was, to be sure, that Etruria grew strong and Rome became the most splendid thing in the world, surrounding her seven hills with a single wall.

Here is the other side of the coin: those qualities and attitudes, which can make the poet, like his rustic people, indifferent to Rome, are the very ones which explain her rise and her greatness. The passages are very close to being in direct contradiction; and yet the poet manages to carry it off with the bravura of his style and the emotional sweep which goes far to unify it all.

In the *Eclogues* the innocent and happy world of the herdsmen was invaded by soldiers and the irresistible power of the state. There is a similar theme in the second half of the *Aeneid*, when the heaven-sent Trojans land in Italy and find themselves in the role of invaders, fighting and killing the local countrymen – 'that humble Italy', as Dante was to say, 'for which the virgin Camilla died, Euryalus, and Turnus, and Nisus, of their wounds' (*Inferno* 1.107-8). This juxtaposition of the idea of the rustic sage who is above patriotism, with the idea of rustic virtue's role in raising Rome to empire, is a sidelight on the same problem in the *Georgics*. Indeed, a question which might have seemed irrelevant to a didactic poem on agricultural techniques was, in reality, at the heart of a poem whose ambitions included a coherent view of life and the position of man in the world; of a poem which was, more specifically, undertaken under the auspices of a dynast who had seized power and who attached importance to a moral revival. What else can Virgil find to say on this most difficult matter?

The vital passages, apart from those already discussed from the Second *Georgic*, are the prologue to the First, the prologue to the Third, and the long mythological narrative which concludes the Fourth. It is an aspect of the unified structure of the poem that its First and Third books begin with long introductions, 42 and 48 lines respectively, in which Maecenas and Octavian are both named. The Second and Fourth, on the other hand, each open with a short paragraph (8 and 7 lines respectively) of simple invocation for the task in hand. There are other structural connections: for instance, the important fact that One and Three both end with long accounts of disaster and death, respectively those of civil war and of plague; that Two ends with praise of the countryman's life; and Four with the enchanting mythological episode of Aristaeus, Orpheus and Eurydice. A suggestive parallel to this alternation of moods would be the movements of a symphony or other extended piece of music.

At the beginning of the *Georgics* Virgil addresses an elaborate and lengthy invocation to the gods and goddesses who patronise agriculture, animals and wild places out of doors (*G* 1.5-23). The surprise for the reader comes in what follows. For the climax of this long list of gods – Bacchus, Ceres, Neptune, Pan, Minerva and the rest – is Octavian, who receives an invocation of the same length (19 lines) as all those regular gods put together. It is still undecided, says the poet, what the special province of this new god is to be. Will he be a god of cities and of the land or perhaps a god of the sea? Perhaps the sea-goddess Tethys will gain him as son-in-law ('buy' him is the word Virgil uses) by offering a bridal gift of all the waters. Or will he join the signs of the Zodiac? Already the Scorpion (the biggest constellation in the Zodiac) is drawing in his claws and leaving him more than his share of the sky. Surely at least he will not choose to be a god of the dead, although it is true that Persephone is happy to stay down there.... At all events, the new god is to help the poet who calls upon him and to grow accustomed to being invoked as divine (*G* 1.24-42).

This, it must be said, is an extremely strange passage. It is true that Julius Caesar had been officially declared a god after his death; but it is hardly possible to believe that Virgil took seriously the idea that his heir would marry a sea-nymph or take his place as a thirteenth sign of the Zodiac. There is a kind of nervous exaggeration about it all, a sense that the poet was perhaps unsure how this new autocrat, whom he had avoided addressing openly in the *Eclogues*, really expected to be handled. The baroque elaboration and bizarreness of the passage must be meant, I believe, to detract from the statement that Octavian is divine, rather than adding to it, since the details are so curious. Romans were not in the habit of addressing living men as gods and, in fact, Octavian soon decided that it was better not to be addressed as one in so direct a way; it is therefore only in the earliest Augustan poems that we find anything comparable.

The man of power makes a startling and not entirely fortunate impact on the beginning of Virgil's poem. And he appears again at the end of the First *Georgic*, at the climax of a harrowing passage on the horrors and crimes of the age. Virgil takes as his starting-point a treatment of the natural signs which will tell a countryman how to predict the weather. This leads him into an emotional account of the natural portents which foretold and accompanied the murder of Caesar. The sin of his murder has been punished by the disastrous battles of the civil war against Brutus and Cassius. In a horrid perversion of good husbandry, 'Roman blood has fertilised the plains of Macedonia'. In time to come the ploughman there will turn up with his ploughshare rust-eaten spears and empty helmets (*G* 1.493-7). Octavian alone can save a world turned upside down: may heaven at least allow him to try:

> hunc saltem everso iuvenem succurrere seclo
> ne prohibete.   (*G* 1.500f.)

These disasters are due to human wickedness, to 'the confounding of right and wrong, to wars and crime everywhere, to the dishonouring of the plough, the ruin of the countryside as the country people are expelled and the ploughshare is melted down to make a sword'. With those words we are back in the world of the First and Ninth *Eclogues*, the world of the evictions, which, as Virgil well remembers, took place on Octavian's orders. The peaceful countryside and the arts of war are in fundamental opposition; in the end peace will prevail (the rusty weapons turned up by the plough). Octavian is the only hope for a world out of control and yet the reminder of the evictions allows an unforgotten shadow to fall even even on him.

The Third *Georgic* opens, as we saw in Chapter 1, with what appears to be a promise by Virgil to produce an encomiastic epic poem on the exploits of Octavian. The ordinary stories of Greek mythology are now all hackneyed, says the poet: how can a singer find a fresh and gripping theme? 'If I live long enough,' he continues, 'I shall lead the Muses home as captives in a triumphal procession; I shall build a temple by the side of the River Mincius [near Mantua]; Octavian shall possess the temple and in his sight I shall conduct games more spectacular than those of Olympia.' On the temple shall be represented in works of art Octavian's past and future conquests; in the niches shall stand statues of his ancestors right back to Troy. 'Soon I shall be girding myself to sing of his brilliant battles' (*G* 3.10-48). Again the passage, like the opening of the First book, is at once profuse and evasive. The image of the Muses following as captives was not one of Virgil's happiest, and it is not clear how his games relate to the pictures on his temple. It is striking that these two passages, so uncharacteristic in their hyperbole and their uneasiness, both relate to Octavian. Virgil has not yet found a satisfactory way of addressing him. We cannot know how far the plan to write an epic on Octavian was seriously meant or worked out by Virgil. What is noteworthy is that the epic which he actually went on to produce was the opposite of what is promised here – not an epic on Octavian with glimpses back to the Trojan ancestors but one on the Trojan ancestors with glimpses forward to their great descendant.

Virgil concluded the *Georgics* in a highly unexpected way. Varro had devoted the last book of his work on agriculture to a wide range of gourmet specialities – the production for the table of fancy fish, birds and game. Enormous profits were being made by the purveyors of pigeons, peacocks, geese, venison, snails, dormice, honey. Virgil reduces all this, with one drastic blow, to honey and bees alone. Sheep and goats were bad enough; snails and dormice would be quite impossible. Bees, on the other hand, though very tiny, are special creatures. They live in an organised and admirable community, often taken as exemplary for human society. Aristotle said that bees had 'something divine about them' (wasps, he rightly added, did not). They produce, in honey, a substance which is incorruptible and capable of symbolic power. And bees, so Virgil supposed, are engendered without sexual intercourse (*G* 4.197ff.). The last is, of course, an effect of the difficulty of making out how bee society works. It was believed until the seventeenth century that the queen was, as Virgil assumes, a king.

Virgil handles his bees with affection. They are 'little Romans' (*parvi Quirites* [*G* 4.201]); they are intensely patriotic, industrious, selfless, dying gladly for the community. 'All have the same rest from work, all have the same toil.' The idle drones are mercilessly expelled from the hive, while 'an inborn love of possession' drives the workers on (*G* 4.177: *innatus apes amor urget habendi*). They die of their hard work but their race goes on for ever. All that is very admirable, no doubt, and it strongly resembles the typical Roman notion of what early Romans were like – not individualists but dour and impersonal, in a favourite phrase of approval 'born not for themselves but for their country'. However, the author of the *Eclogues*, with their glorification of idleness and song, can surely not, we may think, have extolled such a society without reservation; the singer of Corydon and Pasiphae must surely have felt some qualms about expressing unalloyed admiration for creatures for whom sex does not exist. It is suggestive that Virgil makes one omission. Even Varro, by no means a poetical or whimsical writer, refers to the traditional connection of bees and honey with the Muses and with music, calling them 'winged servants of the Muses'. Virgil never makes this allusion; his bees are without the arts. At times he even treats them with evident if straight-faced irony – they *are* awfully small.

We are driven to find some hidden meaning in all this by what follows. Virgil tells a fanciful story about the way to produce new bees if one's own should die. Then, asking 'Who invented this art?', he passes into a long mythical narrative (*G* 4.315-558). Once upon a time Aristaeus, son of the nymph Cyrene, found all his bees dying. He called on his mother for aid and she summoned him into her subterranean residence, the place where all the rivers start. She told him to catch Proteus, the Old Man of the Sea, and ask him the reason for the loss. Held tight in his grasp, the sea-god told the tale: Aristaeus had chased Eurydice (with a view, it appears, to an erotic assault); she, in her flight, was bitten and killed by a snake. Her heartbroken husband Orpheus went down to the lower world to fetch her and, by his power of song, prevailed on the gods of the dead to let her go, provided he did not look back at her until the upper world was regained. But his love overcame him and she was lost a second time. In endless grief, Orpheus rejected the love of other women and, at a Bacchic celebration, a band of them tore him to pieces. It is Orpheus' posthumous anger which Aristaeus must appease. He does so and, by the killing of an ox, succeeds in regaining his bees.

Such is the story. Virgil was the first to say that Orpheus failed to recover his wife; the connection of the story with Aristaeus and with bees was also his invention. What does it mean and why is it an appropriate end to the *Georgics*? It must be said in advance that the episode of Orpheus and Eurydice is told in Virgil's most magical verse:

ipse cava solans aegrum testudine amorem
te, dulcis coniunx, te solo in litore secum,
te veniente die, te decedente canebat.

(G 4.464-6)

Orpheus, trying to comfort his tortured love with his lyre,
sang of you, his sweet wife; of you he sang alone on the shore
of the sea; of you he sang as day came in, of you as day
departed.

The extraordinary accumulation of e-sounds in the last line
presents audibly the dying echoes of his unending monody.
Orpheus, not Aristaeus, is the emotional centre of the story.
Many theories have been put forward about this haunting
episode. Whatever else it may be, it is surely a rare self-
indulgence on Virgil's part – a return to the plangent and
exquisite manner of his youth, to the sensibility which
mourned with Pasiphae, to the decadent poet that Virgil
might have been. The serious purpose of both the *Georgics*
and the subsequent *Aeneid* banished such writing to the
fringes of his work.

My own view is that, in this extraordinary invention,
Virgil was redressing the balance, which the impersonal
society of the bees had swung too far in the direction of
straightforward endorsement of hard work, duty and the
repression of emotions. The bees come back from death,
springing to new life from the corpse of an ox, its mouth and
nostrils stuffed up and its flesh beaten to a pulp through the
unbroken skin (*G* 4.299ff.) – a disconcertingly brutal
remedy, which is supposed to recreate the impersonal soci-
ety of the 'little Romans'. The truly glamorous individuals,
the lover, the musician, Orpheus and Eurydice, are de-
stroyed through Aristaeus' fault and they do not come back;
Orpheus' severed head, floating down the River Hebrus,
still uttered Eurydice's name. A community like that of the
bees has no place for the artist but even death cannot silence

his voice. The tension Virgil felt between the life of the imagination and the constraints of Roman society has found a memorable symbolic utterance.

The *Georgics* end, like the *Eclogues*, with an epilogue of eight lines: 'As I composed my song on crops and trees,' says Virgil, 'Octavian was thundering on the River Euphrates, victorious in war, giving laws to the willing peoples and earning immortality. I, Virgil, was flourishing in the arts of inglorious ease – I who wrote of Tityrus stretched out beneath a spreading beech' (*G* 4.559-66). This most urbane conclusion juxtaposes the activities of the conqueror and ruler, traditionally revered, with the solitary work of the artist, viewed by orthodox Romans as 'inglorious ease'. Virgil appears to accept such a scale of values but he gives himself, not Octavian, the position of climax in this exquisitely balanced paragraph. As with Orpheus, as with the philosophical countryman of the Second *Georgic*, who was unmoved by the fate of the Roman Empire, the poet allows us to hear another voice beneath the superficial acceptance of Octavian and his new Roman order – a voice of the individual sensibility, with its own resources and standards, capable of withdrawing and passing judgement on Rome.

Chapter 4

The *Aeneid* and the myth of Rome

We have seen that Augustus, like other Roman grandees, naturally aspired to have his achievements immortalised in verse. His mastery of propaganda was one of his greatest sources of strength, to which in large part he owed his establishment as the heir of Julius Caesar and his defeat of Mark Antony. Maecenas encouraged the poets whom he patronised to sing the praises of the leader; and Augustus regarded this form of propaganda as sufficiently worthwhile to write letters to Horace, asking why he did not address more poems to him – 'Are you afraid that posterity may hold it against you, if you look like a friend of mine?' – and to Virgil, begging to be shown even a section or an outline of the *Aeneid*. We have quotations from those letters. Yet it would be wrong to think of Augustus as obsessed with these poets or as ascribing too much practical effect to their works. In the extraordinary statement of his own career (*Res Gestae*) which he set up, incised in stone, on his mausoleum he recorded his lavish expenditure on many forms of public benefaction. He refers there to the gladiatorial shows and the athletic contests with which he delighted the people of Rome but there is no word of Horace or of Virgil. He had many other things to do besides reading their productions; for, as Horace put it with an inimitable blend of flattery and irony, addressing Augustus: 'When you alone are shouldering such a weight of affairs, defending the society of Italy in war, adorning it with sound morality and improving it by legislation, I should sin against the public interest if I were to take up your time with a lengthy utterance.' (Horace, *Epistle to Augustus* 1-4).

In the *Georgics* Virgil did address him, in terms which might be accused, without unfairness, of adulation, promising him, at the opening of the Third *Georgic*, an epic poem on his 'brilliant battles' and his conquest of the East. 'The grossest flattery to Augustus that could be invented: the turn of mind in it is as mean as the poetry in it is noble', commented Alexander Pope. I suggested above that the hyperbole is, at least in part, an expression of embarrassment. A self-conscious poet does not find it easy to know how to address a man who was, after all, both an absolute ruler and also a sophisticated person, one not without a sense of humour (some of his jokes are recorded – not perhaps extremely hilarious but they do give evidence that Augustus could be amused and amusing). Virgil now found himself, in the twenties BC, actually turning to the composition of his epic. How was he to go about it?

First, the question of motive. It would be absurd to suppose that Virgil embarked on an epic poem simply in order to flatter Augustus. In his earliest published work he had expressed the aspiration to compose such poetry (*E* 4.53f., 8.7ff.). A widespread doctrine in antiquity held that epic and tragedy were the highest forms of verse, with some feeling that epic was supreme; those who succeeded in the highest forms were the truly great poets. Virgil, conscious of great powers, was naturally moved by the thought of attaining that rank. The time was promising, too; for the old national 'historical' epic (*Annales*) of Quintus Ennius, written more than a hundred years earlier in the infancy of Latin literature, was by now too crude and provincial for the taste of refined contemporaries. Horace, when he mentions Ennius, always has a touch of irony or of direct criticism. The apprenticeship in technique and polish to which Catullus and his friends had subjected Latin verse now opened up the possibility, if there existed a poet of sufficient power, of creating an epic which would be altogether more worthy to represent the greatness of Rome.

Politically, too, although there was the awkwardness of finding an appropriate manner in which to address a Roman autocrat, the perceptible change in the times was in a way alluring. The chaotic and shameful period of civil wars was giving place to the enlightened supremacy of one man, divinely chosen, who would restore peace and order to Rome and the world. That, at least, was the optimistic view, the one already expressed by Virgil in the *Georgics*. It was possible, on the other hand, to view Augustus, and consequently the future, in a much darker light – the uncontrolled domination of a man whose whole career was illegal, whose first act had been to raise an army and march on Rome, who had signed the lists which proscribed innocent citizens, committed unforgotten crimes in the civil wars and climbed to tyranny over the bodies of his enemies and the ruin of the constitution. Virgil must have felt hopes, which were not absurd: after all, Augustus did prove on the whole benign and certainly preferable to any alternative which offered. He must also have felt apprehensions, not only about the ruler's survival (Augustus had weak health and was not expected to live to the great age which he in fact achieved) but also about his intentions. The epic would celebrate his achievement but, at the same time, it would attempt to influence it. Augustus would be shown an image of heroic splendour, moral elevation, true patriotism. Judicious praise – praise of the virtues of a ruler – could be a form of pressure on him to exhibit those very virtues. Virgil was not the last poet to try such means. If, above all, the times really were changing, if this extraordinary man Augustus could save the Empire and reform the world, then to be the laureate of that national revival would be a tremendous thing. The lustre of Virgil's poetry might help to ensure that the revival really took place and that, seeing itself nobly represented in art, it might be transfigured from a mere political coup to a golden age. Something of a similar ambition can be seen in the architecture and the sculpture of the period – a self-conscious striving, with success, for grandeur of style and form.

It is reasonable to suppose that Virgil did give some thought to doing what he seemed to promise in the Third *Georgic*. Could a poet of true artistic conscience produce an epic on the career of Augustus? We can see some of the reasons which led him to decide that it was impossible. The looming presence of Homer meant that a great epic must necessarily be composed in something like the Homeric manner, which was universally felt to be the defining quality of epic poetry. Now the *Iliad* and the *Odyssey* do not simply present their narrative in a high and imposing style. They are set in a world of gods and heroes. Achilles is not just a champion fighter; he is also the son of a goddess, a man whose deeds and sufferings are of immediate and personal interest to all the gods. The Olympians show passionate partisanship for and against Troy, coming down in person to the battlefield and opposing each other in debate and in action. The participation of the divine marks the events as truly significant not only in themselves but as examples of the whole relationship of men with gods, and so with the limits and definition of human life.

All this presented enormous difficulties for a poet who tried to treat recent history and persons, many of whom were still living. Augustus, the heir of Caesar, must be presented as a military leader, whereas everybody knew that he was no swashbuckling warrior. He was ill, so his friends said, at the battle of Philippi; and it was his right-hand man Agrippa who won the victories of the thirties. As for the final battle of Actium, we have observed already that it seems to have been an affair which actually involved very little fighting. To present such engagements ('your brilliant battles') at full length in the Homeric manner was impossible. Could Augustus be described mowing down the enemy with his strong right arm, fighting duels, having personal encounters with divinities? Virgil finally hit on a brilliant solution to the Actium problem, presenting not a narration but a tableau, the central scene on Aeneas' shield (*A* 8.675-713). This allowed him to evade the awkward problems posed by some rather unheroic events and to create a strongly symbolic image – not the shiftiness of civil war but the brilliantly clear outline of a clash between Western civilisation and the barbaric glitter and animal deities of the East: 'Monstrous gods of every shape and the barking dog Anubis' (*A* 8.698).

The divine machinery, too, was a terrible problem. It was all very well to say that Augustus was descended from Venus, and that Apollo favoured his cause at Actium; but could those general ideas be fully unpacked and set out in narrative form? Could Venus appear to him and converse with him, as Thetis does with Achilles or Athena with Odysseus, without bathos and absurdity? A third consideration must have carried no less weight. If the poem was to tell the story of Augustus' career, it must do so in a straightforwardly encomiastic spirit. One can make a case for saying that in the *Iliad* Homer gives the Achaeans the best of it as opposed to the Trojans; but the ethos of the poem is in important respects one of impartiality between them, Hector and his wife and parents being, in some ways, its most sympathetic characters. Virgil would have to commit himself to presenting the whole of recent politics, in some detail, in a nakedly partisan manner, to treating the defeated – not only Brutus and Cassius but also Antony – as villains. Apart from the distasteful crudity of this, some characteristically Virgilian emotions would have to be excluded.

There would be no room for the expression of ambivalence, no room for pathos. Cleopatra, who had now been officially defined as a horrid monster of menace and depravity, could not be seen in the same sympathetic light as Dido. And there could be no moral complexity in the depiction of Rome, of power and conquest. Only enthusiastic endorsement, quite free of undertones or overtones, would serve in a poem expressly devoted to the praise of the great Roman who now ruled the world.

All these considerations must have conspired to induce Virgil to write something quite different. His keen eye saw the one subject which would allow a poet to combine the brilliance of the Greek mythology, its range and dignity, with the one real myth ever produced and believed in by Romans – the myth of Rome herself. By a fortunate chance Augustus, as the adopted son of Julius Caesar, belonged to an ancient aristocratic family which for many years had claimed to be descended from the Trojan hero Aeneas, the son of the goddess Aphrodite (in Latin, Venus). That provided a link with the world to which the epic manner was appropriate; for Aeneas was actually a character in the *Iliad*. There were many stories in circulation about the origins of Rome, their picturesqueness and fullness of detail betraying most of them as essentially Greek in origin. When they encountered a non-Greek people with some signs of civilisation, the Greeks often gave them a kind of honorary half-status by saying that they descended, if not from Greeks, at least from Trojans. It was an extra advantage that the fall of Troy served to explain their turning up in remote places; it served to confirm that they had been forced to leave home. And the non-Greeks concerned, flattered at receiving the entrée into the privileged circle of peoples involved in the great cycles of myth, accepted such stories. More than a hundred years earlier the Elder Cato had said in his *History of Rome* that Aeneas and his Trojans came to

Latium. His version of the story, however, indicates another kind of difficulty for Virgil. According to Cato, the Trojans were plundering the countryside, when the local people gave battle under their king, Latinus, who was killed. That the ancestor and namesake of the Latins should have been killed by the Trojans was unacceptable and Virgil found himself driven to the expedient of making King Latinus an elderly and ineffective ruler who looks on unhappily as younger and more violent men do the fighting. At the end of the *Aeneid* he remains alive to make a union with Aeneas. That detail can stand as representative of a considerable number of difficulties which Virgil found in the various versions of the myth.

By making his epic the story not of Augustus but of Aeneas, Virgil had a ready way to combine the three strands of plot which he regarded as vital: the story of the foundation of Rome from Troy, by a hero famous for his *pietas* (in English something like 'sense of duty', but a considerably more emotional quality for Romans); the history of Rome; and the deliverance of Rome achieved by Augustus. The Trojan story showed the Romans as the equals (in antiquity and heroism) of the Greeks and the foundation of their city as the direct work of heaven –a theme worthy of epic verse. Subsequent Roman history, to be included in the poem in a calculated series of prophetic allusions and revelations, served as a guarantee that the hand of heaven had always accompanied Rome, thus confirming the story of its foundation, while also serving as an inspiration for the future. Augustus is the climax of that history, a second Aeneas; the two figures are made by Virgil to reflect and to resemble each other. The genealogical link between them points up their resemblance and serves, too, as a reciprocal guarantee for each of them: Augustus is the destined leader as the heir of Aeneas, while Aeneas is credible because of the unique greatness of his descendant.

However, mythological speculation did not stop at the Trojan legend. The existence of Rome was also ascribed to another founder, Romulus and the researches of scholars had by this time agreed, to the general satisfaction, that Rome was founded in the eighth century BC. That date was fixed by a sequence of seven kings before the establishment of the Republic in 510 BC. The fall of Troy, however, was generally dated to the twelfth century, 1184 being the most generally favoured date. This left a gap of some centuries, which writers before Virgil had filled up by making Aeneas and his Trojans found, not Rome, but an earlier city nearby – Lavinium. In Virgil's poem it will be Lavinium which Aeneas settles, an ancient town on the coast, some twenty miles south of Rome; then his son will found Alba Longa, another site rich in tradition, half way between Lavinium and Rome, the traditional home of the Julian family. Only after many generations will Romulus at last found Rome.

This aspect of the myth is, at first glance, unsatisfactory. After all the tribulations of the *Aeneid*, Rome still lies in the distant future. Aeneas is the founder of Rome only at a considerable remove. It is interesting to see Virgil at work, first imposing order and shape on material which essentially had none; for Aeneas and Romulus simply come out of different traditions and have no real relationship in time. Early in the poem he makes Jupiter prophesy the course of events: Aeneas will found the first stronghold and reign for three years; his son will found Alba Longa and be king for thirty years; for three hundred years the Trojan race shall rule there, until Romulus founds Rome and names its people after himself –Romans:

> his ego nec metas rerum nec tempora pono:
> imperium sine fine dedi.   (*A* 1.278-9)

> To them I set no limit in space or time: empire I have given
> them without end.

With great skill Virgil creates a passage which might have been no more than a conscientious catalogue of mythological data into a crescendo: three, thirty, three hundred – infinity. The jagged pebbles of the tradition are built into a shape with the appearance of inevitability.

This is just one piece of artistry on a small scale. It does not exhaust the poet's success in transforming what might have been a drawback into an asset. So it is part of the cruelty of Aeneas' destiny that he must sacrifice everything to the god-given task of founding Rome and yet that he will not be allowed to do it. He must take it all on trust up to the end. It is in harmony with this that the whole poem is studded with utterances and omens which predict the future, made by gods, by prophets, in dreams, by the occurrence of symbolic events. This has the effect of making the divine will constantly perceptible as active in events. Nothing happens by chance in the world of the *Aeneid*. It also shows the necessity for Virgilian man to be pious, to be alert for indications of that divine will and responsive and obedient to it.

Virgil has created, in his Eighth book, a poignantly symbolic representation of the destiny of Aeneas. Having finally reached Italy, he finds himself forced to fight a savage war with the Italians. He goes in quest of allies to the old king Evander, who has a little settlement at the foot of the Palatine, on the site which one day will be that of Rome. The hero is entertained in pastoral simplicity and awoken by the song of birds (8.454-67); he is shown the site of the future city, with cows grazing where the Forum will be (it is an irony unsuspected by Virgil that in the Middle Ages they would graze there again and the place be called *Campo Vaccino* – the cattle field). The Roman reader has a moment of rather sentimental pleasure in the reflection that, where now everything is urban and impressive, it was once open country. Yet, beyond that, Virgil adds a deeper note when he asserts that on the hill of the Capitol ('gilded now, but once inaccessible with brambles') already the country people believed that there dwelt a mighty god and the place was viewed with religious awe (8.346ff.). That was to be the site of the great temple of Capitoline Jupiter. The easy nostalgic pleasure of the contrast between sophistication and simplicity is complicated by the sense that this really was a supernatural place, then as now. In addition we feel the pathos of Aeneas, who is going through such sufferings to create Rome, being given only this indirect glimpse of it, unrecognisable but tantalising. In a similar way, at the end of the same book, he is given the marvellous shield forged by Vulcan, sees on it the scenes from Roman history which the god has wrought, and stands gazing at them:

> talia per clipeum Volcani, dona parentis,
> miratur, rerumque ignarus imagine gaudet
> attollens umero famamque et fata nepotum.
>
> (A 8.729-31)

> He gazed in wonder at all this, the work of Vulcan, the gift of his mother: ignorant of the stories, he took pleasure in their representation, and lifted on his shoulder the glory and the destiny of his descendants.

Here the pathos of the pioneer, who must work for a result which he will never see, is yet more powerful than in the figure of the hero visiting the still rustic scene which will be Rome. He is allowed to see the glories of the history which will be, depicted in cold and glittering metal, but, since that history has not yet happened, even with divine aid the hero cannot really understand it. He finds some pleasure in contemplating its uncomprehended image but he must feel its full weight when he carries on his shoulder the brilliant burden of destiny.

In the account of the *Aeneid* presented in this volume I have laid more emphasis on the ideas of the poem, on its structure and significance than on the sensual character of the verse. However, the *Aeneid* would not, of course, have attained and preserved its rank as the supreme poem of Latin literature by its ideas alone. It is also the most beautiful poem in the language, rich and varied in every aspect of style, rhythm and sound.

The hexameter as used by Virgil revealed hitherto unsuspected range and variety. Catullus' short epic (poem 64) on Peleus and Thetis is mellifluous and exquisite but there is a strong tendency to repeat a limited range of rhythmic patterns and to use sequences of end-stopped lines which are static and which would become intolerable in a poem of anything like the length of the *Aeneid*. Virgil exploits every aspect of the earlier technique – the scrupulously controlled rhythms, the resonant epithets, the touches of Greek poetic erudition. For him, however, they are only one element in a style capable of very different effects. It is interesting to compare the opening of Catullus' poem, which describes the sailing of the ship *Argo* in quest of the Golden Fleece, with Virgil's description, where he certainly had the Catullan passage in mind, of Aeneas and his Trojans sailing up the Tiber (8.86ff.). Catullus has strung a series of exquisite lines, each rhythmically almost a separate entity, like golden beads on a thread, whereas Virgil varies his rhythm and runs the sense on unpredictably from line to line. It is like turning from the style of Marlowe to that of a late play by Shakespeare.

Sound-painting in verse is used by Virgil with great finesse. In Latin verse it could easily get out of hand, and there are lines of Ennius, for instance, which have toppled over into the comical. Virgil generally avoids obtrusive effects though occasionally he lets himself go, as for instance in the highly baroque description of Mount Etna (my italics):

> interdum scopulos avulsaque viscera montis
> erigit eructans, liquefactaque saxa sub auras
> cum gemitu glomerat fundoque exaestuat imo.
> fama est Enceladi semustum fulmine corpus
> urgeri mole hac, ingentemque insuper Aetnam
> impositam ruptis flammam exspirare caminis,
> et fessum quoties mutet latus, intremere omnem
> murmure Trinacriam...

(A 3.575-82)

> At times it belches forth aloft crags and dislodged vitals of
> the mountain, hurling molten rocks through the air with a
> roar and boiling in its inmost heart. The tale is that the giant
> Enceladus, half blasted with the thunderbolt, lies crushed
> beneath this massive weight, and that great Etna, piled above
> him, breathes out fire through shattered vents; as often as
> he changes his position, all Sicily shakes with the sound...

Subtler is an effect like the following, where the god of sleep comes to the helmsman Palinurus as he stands at the tiller and, having vainly tried to seduce him from his duty, plunges him into slumber:

> talia dicta dabat, clavumque adfixus et haerens
> nusquam amittebat oculosque sub astra tenebat.
> ecce deus ramum Lethaeo rore madentem
> vique soporatum Stygia super utraque quassat
> tempora, cunctantique natantia lumina solvit.

(A 5.852-6)

> So spoke Palinurus, and holding tight to the tiller he would
> not let go: he kept his eyes fixed on the stars. Suddenly the
> god brandished over his temples a branch drenched in the
> water of Oblivion and full of the power of the Underworld:
> despite his resistance, his swimming eyes fell shut.

The second line of this passage, with its rhyming verbs at middle and end, hints at the unbroken tenacity of Palinurus; in the last line the unusual rhythm and assonance reflect its gradual loss. Virgil not only goes beyond his predecessors in daring experiments with sound and metre; he takes licences and produces bold effects which were not really emulated by his successors.

One of the traditional ornaments of epic poetry was the simile. We shall see that in the very first simile of the *Aeneid* (1.148-56) Virgil, by comparing a natural event to a scene from human life, reverses the normal Homeric procedure. He is, nonetheless, capable of splendid similes in the traditional style, for instance in the scene when the hated Etruscan tyrant Mezentius is attacked on the battlefield by a multitude of his disaffected people:

> As when a wild boar, who for many years has lived safe among the pines of Mount Vesulus or in the Laurentian marsh, is driven by the teeth of the hounds down from his lofty hills; long he has been fattened in the reedy thickets. He comes among the hunters' nets, he stops short and snorts fiercely and makes his shoulders bristle. No man has the courage to come close in and attack him but they press him with spear-casts and shouts which involve no danger. Even so, of all those who had just cause to hate Mezentius, not one had the spirit to attack him with drawn sword: all assail him with missiles and uproar. As for him, undaunted, he turns slowly to every side, grinding his teeth and shaking off the spears which strike his back.

> (*A* 10.707ff.)

Some similes have a thematic function, like the comparison in book Four of Dido to a wounded deer which is picked up by the actual shooting of a tame deer by Ascanius. Others are visionary, as when in book Two Aeneas, after his mother has shown him the gods destroying Troy, sees an image of the fall of the city – a tall and long-lived ash tree, high in the hills, chopped down by woodmen (*A* 2.626ff.): 'It threatens to fall, shakes its foliage and bows its head until at length it is overcome by its wounds and with a final groan spreads ruin far over the hillside'. The tree is like a dying warrior, a

Trojan one of course (the word I have translated as 'foliage' is *comam*, the primary meaning of which is 'hair'); and, since Troy has not at this moment completely fallen, Aeneas 'sees' a scene which includes the future as well as the present.

Virgil is unsurpassed in his coining of memorable single lines. It is not by chance that he was by far the most frequently quoted of Latin poets in antiquity. He can be epigrammatic:

> una salus victis nullam sperare salutem.
>
> (*A* 2.354)
>
> The one salvation for the defeated is to despair of salvation.

He can convey the essence of a scene or a character, as when Dido says of herself, as she promises protection to the shipwrecked Trojans:

> non ignara mali miseris succurrere disco.
>
> (*A* 1.630)
>
> By suffering hardship myself I have learned to succour those in distress.

It is a line which expresses not only her humanity but also her tact in putting herself on a level with those who find themselves forced to come to her as suppliants. Again, when Aeneas is importuned both by Dido and by her sister Anna to stay in Carthage, Virgil says:

> mens immota manet, lacrimae volvuntur inanes.
>
> (*A* 4.449)
>
> His will remains unmoved, in vain fall his tears.

Other lines are unforgettable for their vividness, as when we read of Aeneas and the Sibyl entering the Underworld:

> ibant obscuri sola sub nocte per umbram...
>
> (*A* 6.268)

In gloom they passed, through the shades of that unpeopled night.

Bold rhythmic effects can work with such lines, like the juxtaposition of long open vowels before a half-rhyming close in a line which depicts the unsatisfied desire of the unburied dead to cross the River Styx:

tendebantque manus ripae ulterioris amore.

(*A* 6.314)

They stretched out their hands in yearning for the further shore.

Again, when Jupiter finally yields to the prayer of Juno that the Italians shall not be forced to become Trojans, he does so in a line which begins with a series of long slow mono-syllables, then runs out in a freer and more relaxed rhythm:

do quod vis et me victusque volensque remitto.

(*A* 12.833)

I grant what you wish: both overcome and willingly I yield.

Virgil is capable of splendid rhetoric, as for instance in the hate-filled debating speeches with which Venus and Juno assail each other on Olympus at the beginning of book Ten, or the powerful and angry exchange between Turnus and Drances, an Italian who wishes to make peace with Aeneas, in book Eleven (343ff.). These are speeches of a more or less political character. The power of rhetoric appears on a more intimate scale in the last utterances of Dido. Here she wishes that she had slaughtered Ascanius and attacked the Trojans in war (my italics):

verum anceps pugnae *f*uerat *f*ortuna. *f*uisset:
quem *m*etui *m*oritura? *f*aces in castra tuli*ss*em
imple*ss*emque *f*oro*s f*lammis natumque patremque
cum genere exstinx*em*, *mem*et super ipsa dedi*ss*em.

(*A* 4.603-6)

> But the outcome of battle would have been uncertain. So let
> it be! What man had I to fear, when I was doomed anyway?
> I could have set his camp ablaze, filled his decks with fire,
> wiped out father and son and all their race, and thrown myself
> on top of the pyre.

The alliteration, especially the hissing s-sounds, lend power
and panache to this outburst of solitary hate. At the opposite
extreme Virgil can rise to the most majestic utterance of the
king of the gods. Jupiter's speech to Venus (1.257ff.) is in
the very grandest style, delivered by the god with a smile on
'the face which brings calm to sky and tempest' (*vultu quo
caelum tempestatesque serenat* [255]).

The suppleness of which his speeches are capable can be
illustrated by Dido's last words. She has built a pyre for
herself and, reclining upon it on the bed in which she had
been united with Aeneas, she is about to stab herself with
Aeneas' sword:

> 'dulces exuviae, dum fata deusque sinebat,
> accipite hanc animam meque his exsolvite curis.
> vixi et quem dederat cursum Fortuna peregi,
> et nunc magna mei sub terras ibit imago.
> urbem praeclaram statui, mea moenia vidi,
> ulta virum poenas inimico a fratre recepi,
> felix, heu nimium felix, si litora tantum
> numquam Dardaniae tetigissent nostra carinae.'
> dixit, et os impressa toro 'moriemur inultae,
> sed moriamur' ait. 'sic, sic iuvat ire sub umbras.
> hauriat hunc oculis ignem crudelis ab alto
> Dardanus, et nostrae secum ferat omina mortis.'

> (*A* 4.651-62)

'Beloved tokens while fate and heaven allowed, receive my
spirit and rid me of my pain. I have lived my life and acted
out to the end the course that fortune allotted, and now a
proud ghost of what I am shall pass under the earth, I have
founded a noble city, I have seen my city's walls, I have

> punished my hostile brother and avenged my husband:
> happy, all too happy alas! if only the Trojan ships had never
> touched my shore.' Then she kissed the bed and said, 'I shall
> die unavenged, but let me die. Thus, thus, do I go gladly to
> join the shades. Let the cruel Trojan from mid-ocean drink
> in the sight of this pyre and carry with him the evil omen of
> my death.'

Dido begins on a tender note of regret for past happiness
in the first two lines. She goes on, with a change of mood,
to say that her life has been one on which she can look with
pride: first that is stated in general terms, then spelt out in
a way which deliberately recalls the style of the epitaphs of
Roman grandees listing their achievements (655-6). Then
another revulsion of feeling: if only Aeneas had not come
along and ruined it all! A softer, more plaintive tone makes
itself heard, as after the lapidary statement of her public
achievements comes the feeling of private unhappiness and
blighted love. Kissing the bed is a gesture of farewell to life
suitable to a married woman (what Dido claimed to be); in
the context of suicide and a curse on the man she loved it
expresses the inextricable entanglement of love and hate.
With the repeated *sic* ('thus') we hear the actual thrust as
she stabs herself, claiming to be glad to die. She is on the
bed she shared with Aeneas; she holds *his* sword; yet she will
not speak his name even in a curse (he is 'the Trojan'). The
whole speech, short as it is, conveys the complex and con-
flicting emotions of the heroine with impeccable sureness
of touch.

A final aspect of Virgil's style which should be touched
on is his pathos. In what follows a number of examples are
discussed, but the quality is so characteristic of him that it
deserves to be explicitly singled out here. We find unobtru-
sive touches, as when the young prince Lausus, killed in
battle by Aeneas, is stabbed 'through the tunic which his
mother had embroidered with gold thread' (10.818), a

detail which brings out his youth, his mother's loving care, the handsome figure that he had been. For the funeral of the young prince, Pallas Aeneas sends two cloaks of crimson, embroidered with gold, 'which once Dido had made for him, happy at her work' (11.73-4). The two words *laeta laborum* repay lingering: they show us, as at that moment they show Aeneas, the happiness he has lost with the woman who loved him. Her gifts can appropriately go now to the dead.

In book Five the Trojan women disgrace themselves by attempting to burn the ships in Sicily so that Aeneas will have to stay there and not press on still further to Latium. Aeneas agrees to leave them (and such of the men as want to go no further) in Sicily with King Acestes. But when the time comes for Aeneas and the others to sail on: 'Then there was weeping on the shore and embracing. Even the women, even the men who had found the sea cruel and heaven's command unbearable, now wish to go on and to endure any suffering of the journey. Kindly Aeneas comforts them with loving words.' (5.765ff.). That is a profound piece of human nature.

The episode of Dido is a masterpiece of the pathetic; and the second half of the *Aeneid* is pervaded by touching deaths. One last passage can be singled out here. When they arrive in Africa, Aeneas and his associate Achates are concealed in mist by the goddess Venus. So concealed, they make their way to Dido's palace. The first building they find is a temple, in which Dido has placed pictures representing scenes from the Trojan War. Aeneas gazes fascinated and weeps at the sight of their past sufferings (1.460ff.): 'What part of the world is not full of our sorrows? Look, there is Priam! Even here glory has its reward: there are tears for history and human sufferings touch the heart.' (*sunt lacrimae rerum et mentem mortalia tangunt*, [456ff.]). Sharing in the sorrows of others guarantees humanity and gentle treatment and sure enough Dido, when she appears, says that by suffering herself she has learned pity. Pity is the English word derived from the Latin *pietas* and pity is as characteristic of the poem as *pietas* is of its hero. It will not have escaped the reader that in every one of these cases it is the impulsion of the gods which produces the pitiful scenes and pathetic language.

After these preliminary remarks it is time to turn to the structure of the poem in closer detail. It tells of the career of Aeneas, who survives the sack of Troy and is given by the gods the glorious but exacting task of transferring the Trojan gods to Italy and establishing there a community which shall one day found the city Rome, which will rule the world. In the first six books the wanderings of the hero recall the *Odyssey*, while in the second half the fighting in Italy recalls the *Iliad*. In each half, however, important episodes derive from the other Homeric epic (thus the Funeral Games in the Fifth book exploit those in *Iliad* 23, while Aeneas' visit to Evander in the Eighth book recalls that of Telemachus to Nestor in *Odyssey* 3). The story is essentially a very simple one, but it is adorned and complicated with a vast range of episodes, with echoes and motifs from Greek tragedy, later Greek poetry, Ennius, Lucretius, Roman history, and various ideas from Virgil's reading in geography, philosophy and theology.

The poem opens with a weighty invocation and prologue.

> I sing of war and a man, whose destiny brought him in exile from Troy to the shore of Lavinium, much battered on land and sea by the violence of gods, because of cruel Juno's unrelenting anger: in war, too, he suffered greatly before he could found his city and bring his gods to Latium, the origin of the Latin people and the Alban fathers and the towering walls of Rome. Tell me, Muse, the reasons: for what injury or what grievance the queen of heaven made a hero outstanding for *pietas* undergo such sufferings and such toils. Do heavenly spirits feel such passions?   (*A* 1.1-11)

That opening deliberately recalls Homer's invocations. What exactly the Muse meant to Virgil we cannot know, but I do not think she is a mere poetical cliché. The inspiration that comes from the Muse is an image for the essentially mysterious nature of great poetry, which cannot be explained by an account of the rational work that has gone into it. After the statement of the theme and the allusion to 'cruel Juno', the poet departs from the objective manner, traditional in Homeric epic, in which the personality of the singer is not revealed. He turns to a more evidently emotional style, asking the Muse, in the traditional way, to tell him about things which are not accessible to mortal inspection. Here he presses the question in an untraditional direction: how can a great goddess have treated in this unjust way a man outstanding for moral virtue? It is as if Virgil were shocked by his own story when he goes on with the remonstrance: *can* gods really feel such passions?

As everywhere in the *Aeneid*, the juxtaposition of the orthodox with the new is what produces the characteristic Virgilian atmosphere. Homer had asked the Muses to tell him such things as the number of the Achaean warriors engaged in battle or the name of the first man to kill an opponent. Virgil asks not for a fact but for a justification. The strong passions and unashamed partisanship of the Homeric gods had shocked serious thinkers for generations. Virgil allows that vein of moral criticism into the epic itself. At 1.36 the goddess Juno will appear, expressing her enmity for Troy because of some personal grievances of an unedifying character: the Trojan prince Paris, in the beauty contest of the three goddesses, denied her the prize; the Trojan boy Ganymede was beloved by her husband Jupiter. She sees Aeneas and his men sailing westwards and she bribes the god of the winds to unleash a fearful storm. So the answer to Virgil's sorrowful question is apparently 'Yes: heavenly spirits do know such human rage'. But the prominent position in which the question is put, and the absence of an answer, leave it echoing in the reader's mind. The function of Juno and her hostility is to delay the founding of Lavinium and to cause suffering to Aeneas. As Virgil says, after summing up the effects of the anger of the goddess (1.22-32):

tantae molis erat Romanam condere gentem.

(*A* 1.33)

So great the toil it cost to found the nation of Rome.

At the level of myth, personal grudges of a powerful goddess caused suffering to Aeneas. But that level is, from the beginning of the poem, not above question. At another level, the cost of imperialism is high: there is something in heaven which has always made the Roman pay dearly for it. Aeneas, in the *Aeneid*, must leave his country, abandon Dido, massacre Italians, renounce the arts for the hard and lonely destiny of conquest and rule (6.847-53). Virgil's remonstrance at this harshness seems to go beyond the familiar criticism of the all-too-human gods of the old mythology and become a plea, poignantly unanswered, against the logic of imperialism itself. Not only here but throughout the *Aeneid* the divine machinery of Jupiter and the other gods presents difficulties; the Homeric deities had for centuries been attacked for their levity and immorality. For Virgil they also offered a great opportunity for suggesting complexities which he prefers not to make too explicit. The grand pronouncements and long views of Jupiter, his moral injunctions and his patronage of Rome are juxtaposed with accounts of his own light-hearted violations of nymphs (we shall discuss this question later) as well as with passages of 'philosophical' doctrine, like that of Anchises at 6.724ff. The latter are evidently of a different origin and nature and they account for the world in a way which suggests a kind of pantheism – a universally pervasive divine spirit in all things – rather than personal gods and goddesses. The implication seems to be that the divine motivation of events should not be taken too literally. Virgil exploits the moral vulnerability of the other gods in the same way. Juno's angry passions are in a way impressive. They conform to a classic conception of the behaviour of gods in poetry; but another voice in the poem calls them into question, at least as factually true; and the unbridged gap between the two conceptions adds to the pathos of a destiny which certainly involves suffering, labour and guilt, not only for Aeneas but also for the Roman people whose symbol he is. The reasons for that suffering, though explained, remain essentially mysterious (as suffering always is mysterious in reality), so making his account both more pathetic and more profound than one seen from a traditional approach. To achieve it, Virgil has exploited the old conventions of poetry in a new way.

In this episode Juno succeeds. She bribes Aeolus to let loose the winds. One ship is lost and the others are in peril, when Neptune, god of the sea, intervenes to check this invasion of his prerogative. Winds and waves are stilled, and Virgil uses a striking comparison:

> 'As when a mob is raging and out of control but, at the sight of some man whose *pietas* and public services lend him authority, falls into respectful silence. His utterance calms their angry passions. Even so did the sea become tranquil at the appearance of the god.'

> (*A* 1.148ff.)

This is the first simile in the poem. Such elaborate comparisons are one of the most striking features of the Homeric poems; and the *Aeneid*, as a poem in the Homeric tradition, includes some very fine ones. But here Virgil has reversed the Homeric procedure: instead of illustrating human events by comparison with those of nature (Homer actually compares a rowdy assembly to a stormy sea at *Iliad* 2.144), a storm at sea is compared to a political scene – and a very Roman one at that. The great man whose authority prevails is an ideal Roman figure. So with this first simile Virgil again shows the perceptive reader how his poem will combine Greek and Roman, traditional and original.

The Trojans were sailing from Sicily to Italy; that is to say they were near their goal. The storm scatters them and drives them on to the coast of Africa and so into the entanglement with Dido, queen of Carthage. Poor Aeneas, though himself much disheartened (his first words are a wish that he had died at Troy, 1.94-6), consoles and feeds his crew. The rest of the ships have disappeared and he does not know if they have survived. Now the scene moves to heaven. Aeneas' mother Venus appeals to Jupiter: is this the way the promised destiny is fulfilled? Jupiter reassures her. Fate is unchanged. He reveals the future – the rise and the endless rule of Rome. The descendants of Troy shall subjugate and rule over their Greek conquerors. A Julius shall be borne descended from Aeneas' son Ascanius (also called Iulus), who shall rule the world and become a god. In his day war shall cease (1.257-96). This Julius is Augustus but Virgil has preferred to leave a slight haze of ambiguity by calling him by the name which not only links him with Aeneas but also evokes his adoptive father, Julius Caesar, already deified, as a kind of guarantee that Augustus too will reach heaven. This utterance by Jupiter is programmatic: whatever happens later in the poem we are to retain the memory that in the end all will be well.

Meanwhile Aeneas has met his mother, who appears to him disguised as a local girl. The hero complains bitterly: *sum pius Aeneas* ('I am the dutiful Aeneas: and look how I am treated, shipwrecked and lost in Africa'). The goddess, having told him where he is and what to expect from Dido, rebukes him for his complaints. Suddenly, as she leaves him, her beauty, her perfume and her motion change to reveal her true identity. Aeneas calls after her, begging her to stay: 'Why do you constantly deceive your son with false appearances? You are as cruel as the rest of them! Why can I never touch your hand and have a real conversation with you?' (1.402ff.). The scene is again programmatic. Aeneas is the son of a goddess but she is not a real mother to him, as Thetis is to Achilles in the *Iliad*. She does not allow him even the companionship that Odysseus gets from Athena. The gods care for Aeneas because the plans of destiny need him; his own happiness does not seem to concern them. The favoured hero is lonely and comfortless.

He makes his way to the court of Dido, a noble figure, who fled from her brother when he murdered her husband and who is now founding Carthage. A beautiful widowed queen with a tender heart, she is the right wife for the widower Aeneas, even without divine intervention. Yet it is Juno and Venus who conspire, for very different motives, to force the issue. Juno hopes to keep Aeneas in Carthage, so that Rome will never come into existence; Venus wants Dido to be nice to her son. Venus substitutes the boy-god Cupid for Aeneas' son: the childless Dido holds him on her lap and the god inspires her with the passion which in any case would have been natural. The behaviour of the goddesses must, I think, be felt as a very dirty trick. Venus favours Aeneas only because he is her son – that is, for personal reasons not so different from those of Juno for hating him. Light-heartedly she gets him into a fearful difficulty.

The Second and Third books contain the recital by Aeneas of his adventures from the fall of Troy to his landing in Africa. The structural model is Odysseus' account of his adventures to the Phaeacians in *Odyssey* 9-12. Here there is, however, the added point that, whereas the Phaeacians simply listened with pleasure to marvellous stories, Dido falls in love, like Desdemona, as she hears Aeneas tell of the dangers he has passed. In the Second book Virgil describes the taking of Troy – a most ambitious venture. Such scenes as the killing of Priam had often been represented in poetry and art; so Virgil challenged hard comparisons. He has the particular difficulty, too, that Aeneas survived the destruction of his country and sailed away with a considerable body of men. That was not obviously heroic and, indeed, some versions of the story had made him a traitor. Virgil emphasises two things. First, the doom of Troy was fixed and unavoidable. Aeneas is repeatedly given divine portents and explicit warnings to that effect. Hector in a dream, his goddess mother in person, a Trojan priest who hands over to his care the household gods of Troy – all tell him to go and to perpetuate Troy overseas. Second, it is stressed that Aeneas is very unwilling to accept these instructions. He rushes off to fight and die; so the gods have to send another explicit sign, a supernatural flame around the head of his son, before he will leave the burning city. He is not less than Homeric in his heroism. He has all the old-style heroic fighting spirit and scorn of death but, in addition, he must learn to accept submission to the far-reaching purposes of heaven.

Aeneas leaves Troy, carrying his old father Anchises and leading his young son by the hand. His wife Creüsa follows at a distance and, when he arrives at the rendezvous outside the town, she has vanished. She appears to him, with supernatural stature, to tell him that she is kept behind by the gods in Troy, but that he is to sail to Italy and the River Tiber: 'There prosperity and a kingdom await you, and a princess as your bride' (2.783). The episode is an extraordinary one. Making Aeneas' wife predict his new bride is a cruel stroke and, although Aeneas exhibits the appropriate emotions, it is hard entirely to evade a feeling that the ideal Virgilian family is that which has now been created by her removal –

grandfather, father, son. The question of women in the
Aeneid is indeed a curious one, which will repay a moment's
consideration. There are no happy families in the *Aeneid*
(the domesticity of Aeneas and Creüsa is seen only in the
desperate scenes of the fall of Troy) and women are, on the
whole, alarming and violent creatures, prone to the making
of terrible scenes. Compare for instance the dignified grief
of Evander for his son with the uncontrolled shrieks of
Andromache and of Euryalus' mother, who by her wailings
breaks the morale of the troops (11.152ff.; 3.306-9; 9.480-
502). Creüsa is left in Troy; the other Trojan matrons run
wild in Sicily and try to burn the ships (they even snatch
consecrated fire from the altar for their unhallowed pur-
pose) and they are left behind in Sicily (5.613ff.). Lavinia's
mother goes crazy and in the end hangs herself. Dido
becomes violent and alarming. And there is always the
terrible goddess Juno. It is tempting to see in all this the
expression of a sensibility to which heterosexual love made
comparatively little appeal. But it should be added that
Virgil has tried to make this sensibility serve the main
purposes of his epic. For in being deprived by the exigencies
of destiny of the normal emotional satisfactions of a man,
Aeneas symbolically accepts the hard and lonely lot of the
imperialist.

Despite the unambiguous naming of the Tiber at the end
of the Second book, in the Third book the Trojan refugees
have no idea where they are supposed to go and they try a
series of places in vain gradually acquiring more details
about their goal as they travel. There is other evidence,
besides apparent ignorance of Creüsa's prophesy, to suggest
that this book is further than any other part of the poem
from being in its final form: it contains only one simile; also
the only unfinished line in the poem which fails to complete
the sense (3.340); the chronology presents difficulties; and
in places the style is rather below the general level of the

Aeneid. But it does contain effective scenes notably a pathetic encounter with Andromache, Hector's widow, who together with another Trojan survivor, Helenus, has set up a tiny replica of Troy in Epirus and lives in the past, thinking only of the husband and son she has lost (3.296ff.). That road, a lachrymose and petrified nostalgia, is a temptation to be resisted and Aeneas goes on, revealing his emotions in his parting words: 'Live in happiness, you whose destiny is already accomplished! You have achieved peace while we are driven on from one fatality to another, ploughing the sea and following the fields of Italy which constantly recede before us.' (3.493ff.). The last and greatest of Aeneas' sufferings is the death of his father, taken from him in Sicily, when the Trojans have finally learned that it is the Tiber they must make for.

The Fourth book belongs to Dido. She is given eight speeches in the book, while Aeneas has only one. She is in the grip of a violent passion for him, which leads her to roam the city like a deer, wounded with an arrow by a countryman who does not know he has hit her (4.68ff.). She even neglects the work of building her new city. Here Virgil faced an apparently insuperable difficulty, which he has solved with brilliant panache. On the one hand, Dido is a dignified and serious character who cannot simply embark on a commonplace intrigue; on the other, Aeneas cannot be shown deserting a wife. Virgil creates what seems impossible, a situation which is ambiguous between marriage and non-marriage. Out on a hunting expedition the two are caught in a storm. They take refuge together in a cave. Juno, who is goddess of marriage, has planned all this. She has said that they will be married (4.126) and, as they enter the fateful cave:

> prima et Tellus et pronuba Iuno
> dant signum; fulsere ignes et conscius aether
> conubiis, summoque ulularunt vertice Nymphae.
>
> (*A* 4.166-8)

Primordial Earth and Juno of marriage gave the signal; lightning flashed and the sky was witness to their nuptials, while the Nymphs raised a cry on the mountain peak.

The goddess of marriage presides; the lightning flashes and the shrieking of the Nymphs represent the torches and the ritual cries of a Roman wedding. Dido called this, says Virgil, a wedding – and clearly not without some grounds. Yet when Aeneas is challenged by her, he can say with truth that he never went through a proper marriage ceremony (4.338-9). All the same, we are meant to feel that this is less than a complete exculpation. After the incident in the cave he lives with Dido openly, wearing a cloak of crimson and gold which she has embroidered for him and actually joining her in founding, not Rome, but Rome's subsequent arch-enemy – Carthage (4.260ff.). He has sailed very close to the wind.

Jupiter intervenes with shattering effect, sending Mercury with a peremptory message to Aeneas. The hero, aghast, plans an inconspicuous departure, 'while the excellent Dido knew nothing and had no thought that their great love was being broken off' (4.291-2). He plans to tell her when the right moment comes along. Naturally this typically masculine strategy does not work and he finds himself overwhelmed by her reproaches and pleas. He is slow to answer and what he has to say (*A* 4.333-61) is repressed and not likely to satisfy Dido: he will always be grateful for her help; he did not plan to leave without telling her; he never married her; he is leaving under duress. If he had his own choice, he says tactlessly, he would have stayed in Troy and rebuilt the city; it is the gods who order him away. 'Do not work us both up with your tears – it is not by my will that I sail for Italy' (4.360-1). The reader is not meant to feel that Aeneas does not love Dido – when she collapses at the end of her next speech of passionate denunciation, he 'groans, his heart shaken by the greatness of his love' (4.395) – but the spotlight is on her emotions, not on his. And he, not for the only time in the poem, is inarticulate (at 4.390 he is said to be 'hesitating and having much to say' but he does not succeed in expressing it). He carries out the divine orders and sails away, while Dido delivers a series of powerful rhetorical speeches expressing the whole gamut of emotions – rage, shame, scorn, hatred, remorse, revenge, pride, despair. Greek tragedy, especially the *Medea* of Euripides, was important for Virgil here; also the *Argonautica* of Apollonius of Rhodes, a Greek poet of the third century BC. The effect is akin to grand opera, in some ways, rather than to Homer or to Shakespeare. It is characteristic of the *Aeneid* that it contains many speeches but little conversation or exchange of ideas. Dido's utterances are like a series of arias for an unhappy operatic heroine. Eventually she kills herself, invoking eternal enmity between Carthage and Rome. The wars with Carthage were the most terrible that Rome ever fought and Virgil has succeeded in linking that unforgotten crisis with his mythical story.

The total significance of the Dido episode requires us to look ahead to the scene in book 6 (450ff.) where Aeneas, in the world of the dead, has to confront her ghost in the region peopled by those who died for love. He assures her again that he did not want to leave her and he begs her to speak to him. She keeps an unbroken and angry silence, her eyes fixed on the ground, then turns away and vanishes into the gloom, leaving the hero to watch her go, tears of pity in his eyes. Ancient literature, in contrast with Christian writing, is not much interested in forgiveness. At the end of the *Iliad* Achilles, having killed Hector, refuses to surrender his corpse for burial and, in the ecstasy of hatred, drags it behind his chariot. Finally the gods intervene: Zeus sends Hector's father, King Priam, into Achilles' presence to ransom the body. Achilles is moved by the sight of the aged king kneeling at his feet and kissing the hand that killed his son. Together the two men weep, Priam for Hector, Achilles for his dead friend Patroclus and for his own old father, who resembles Priam in age and in unhappiness. At last Achilles speaks: 'This is the cruel lot of mankind, and there is no man to whom Zeus does not allot suffering'.

That scene, with all its poignancy a high point of Homeric poetry (and one often depicted in art), Virgil could not use. The unimportance of nationality in the perspective of life and death is a perception which could find no place in what is, after all, a nationalistic poem. But it is worth observing, for our present purpose, that there is between Achilles and Priam no question of forgiveness. What they share is a moment of insight into the nature of human life. The last encounter of Aeneas and Dido is one of the few important scenes in ancient literature which hinge on forgiveness – forgiveness requested by Aeneas, denied by Dido. The destiny of Rome was splendid but it involved the destruction of many attractive things and the ruin of the innocent. That is an inescapable part of imperialism and the supreme price of empire is that it makes you into an imperialist. Aeneas' coming has destroyed Dido. As she says just before her suicide, she was 'all too happy, if only the Trojan fleet had never come to my coast' (4.657-8). The destruction is final and there is no forgiveness for it. Aeneas meant well but the damage is done; he is left with the guilt. Thus Virgil has contrived to make an episode of tragic love, the worthy successor to his Pasiphae and his Orpheus and Eurydice, into a profound and poignant symbol of the gain and loss of empire. There could be no better example of turning to the service of epic a temperament naturally suited, it might seem, to exquisite minor verse.

The Fifth book brings the Trojans back to Sicily, where Aeneas celebrates his father's funeral games. In the Sixth book he finally reaches Italy and there descends into the Underworld to see his father's spirit. This is a great book, in which the Homeric model of *Odyssey* 11 is enriched with many additions. Not the least surprising aspect of Homer's work is the rationality, the coolness, of his presentation of the world of the dead. Odysseus talks to the ghosts with a keen interest not different, one almost feels, from that which he shows in all the other exotic places in which he finds himself; there are hardly any horrors. Virgil adds monsters, Furies, 'shapes terrible to see' (6.277); the boatman Charon, his eyes ablaze with fire (6.300); and the monstrous three-headed hound Cerberus (6.417). He also strikes the nationalistic note. Anchises shows his son a long line of the Roman heroes who are yet to be born, first two important 'founders', Romulus and then Augustus:

> hic vir, hic est, tibi quem promitti saepius audis,
> Augustus Caesar, divi genus, aurea condet
> saecula qui rursus Latio regnata per arva
> Saturno quondam, super et Garamantas et Indos
> proferet imperium.   (*A* 6.791-5)

> Here, here is the man who has so often been promised to you, Augustus Caesar, son of a god: he shall bring back the golden age in Latium where Saturn ruled of old, and extend the empire over the peoples of Africa and India.

There follow the great names of the Roman Republic, the Scipios, the Fabii and all the rest, the conquerors of the world. With all this, says the poet, his father 'fired the hero's mind with desire for future fame' (6.889).

Yet this simple message is inextricably entwined with very different suggestions. First, when Aeneas catches sight of the unborn souls his reaction is a surprising one: 'Can it be true that some souls ascend from here and return again

to the sluggish body? What perverse desire is this in the poor
creatures for the light of day?' (6.719-21). That plangent
question is not quite what we might expect from the pro-
genitor of a race of conquerors. It reminds us that the hero's
first utterance in the poem is the wish that he were dead. In
reply Anchises expounds a Platonic philosophy of rebirth
after purgatory for sin, which seems to disregard the ques-
tion of nationality altogether (6.724-51). The parade of
Roman heroes is punctuated by passages whose tenor is
plaintive and regretful: Lucius Brutus, the founder of the
Republic, put his own sons to death for conspiring to bring
back the banished king – 'Unhappy man!', cries Anchises,
'However posterity will judge his act: love of country will
prevail, and the limitless desire for glory' (6.822-3). 'Limit-
less desire for glory' is, at best, an uneasy justification for
killing one's own sons and the first hero of the Republic is
to be pitied, whatever posterity has to say. Then (*A* 6.826ff.)
Caesar and Pompey appear: 'Don't do it, my sons! Don't
wage civil war and turn your country's strength against her
own vitals! Throw down the sword!' (832-3) – a pathetic
appeal which we know will not be heeded.

The parade of champions ends with an unexpected
passage (847ff.) in which Anchises says that, while 'others'
(that is, of course, the Greeks) 'will excel in sculpture, in
oratory, in astronomy':

> tu regere imperio populos, Romane, memento
> (hae tibi erunt artes) pacique imponere morem,
> parcere subiectis et debellare superbos.
>
> (*A* 6.851-3)

> Do you, man of Rome, be mindful to rule the nations – these
> shall be your arts – and to impose civilisation after peace:
> spare the defeated and bring down the arrogant in war.

This is a proud claim but also a fearful renunciation. In the
middle of the greatest work of Latin literature Virgil feels

obliged to ascribe to Rome not the sciences and the arts but only the hard and impersonal 'arts' of conquest and rule. That, too, is part of the price of empire. The scene concludes with another outburst of pathos. The last figure to appear is that of Marcellus, Augustus' nephew and intended heir, who had died in 23 BC at the age of nineteen. Twenty-six lines celebrate the precocious promise and tragic death of the young man (6.860-86). That must have pleased the Imperial family; but it also enabled Virgil to close this scene, and the first half of the poem, with lines of mellifluous lamentation:

> heu, miserande puer, si qua fata aspera rumpas,
> tu Marcellus eris. manibus date lilia plenis,
> purpureos spargam flores animamque nepotis
> his saltem accumulem donis, et fungar inani
> munere.   (*A* 6.882-6)

> Alas, unhappy boy: if you can break through fate's cruelty,
> you will be a Marcellus. Bring lilies in armfuls, let me strew
> dark flowers and honour the soul of my grandson with these
> offerings at least, and present my unavailing gift.

The great parade of generals and statesmen ends with loss, defeat, impotent regret. It is not mere twentieth-century suspicion of imperialism which makes us feel that Virgil's message here is by no means simple.

In the Seventh book Aeneas reaches Latium and the River Tiber. 'A greater subject, a greater work begins', says the poet (7.44). Not all readers have agreed: of the twelve books, the Fourth and Sixth remain the most popular. Virgil now describes the war which Juno stirred up against the immigrants in Italy, brought to an end when at last Aeneas kills Turnus, the Italian prince who is his rival for the hand of Lavinia, daughter of old King Latinus – the royal bride who was predicted by Creüsa at the end of the Second book. The Seventh book has clear echoes of the First. Juno appears again – and with another angry monologue (7.293-322). At first she had hoped to destroy the Trojans altogether but now she limits her aim to causing delay and distress. In the First book she invoked the god of the winds to help her; now she is obliged to employ an appalling Fury out of Hell, to whom she seems ashamed to be seen talking. That is what happens to a goddess who opposes the purposes of fate. She cannot be killed like Dido and Turnus but she is driven into a corner. In the end she will have to give up.

The Fury intervenes, when it seemed that all was going well, that Latinus would accept Aeneas as ally and as son-in-law. Amata, Latinus' queen, goes mad with hostility to the new suitor. Turnus is roused to anger. And Aeneas' young son shoots a stag which turns out to be the pet of a local girl. The beautiful wounded deer flees home, bleeding and 'seeming to beg for help' (7.502); and the country people rush to punish the Trojan intruders. It is irresistible to recall Dido, compared to a wounded deer shot by a careless archer. The symbolism in both cases is clear: the god-sent invaders destroy the innocent. There was no intention in either of doing such harm, and yet the harm is done. The book concludes with a catalogue of the Italian peoples who flocked to the war. It was important to Virgil to include in his great epic not only Rome but also Italy – Etruscans, Latins, even Italian Greeks (Evander is a Greek), who each receive sympathy and attention. Rome is not simply an alien power, imposed on everybody else; as we shall see in the Twelfth book, the Italian contribution is vital.

Aeneas, leaving his son in command, goes off to look for allies with those Trojan chieftains who so strikingly fail to become distinct personalities in the poem. The contrast with the rich gallery of individuals in the *Iliad* is indeed great. Virgil, it seems, had little talent for the creation of person-alities. It was, he might argue, precisely part of the destiny of Rome that her people were less individualistic, more uniform than the self-indulgent Greeks. We have already seen that in the Eighth book Aeneas comes to the site of Rome. There King Evander sends his beloved son, the handsome and high-spirited Pallas, to go with Aeneas and to learn from him how to be a hero – a decision that will have terrible consequences.

At the end of the book Aeneas receives a set of armour, made by Vulcan. The shield is described in detail. It is worth making the obvious contrast with Virgil's model, with the marvellous shield which is made for Achilles in the *Iliad* (18.478-609). On the latter the god Hephaestus, Vulcan's Greek counterpart, represented the whole world: 'On it he put earth and sky and sea, the tireless sun and the full moon and all the stars that stud the heaven.' Round the edge was the stream of Ocean, and in the middle were a city at peace and a city at war, a wedding, a law-suit, a battle, ploughing and reaping, boys and girls dancing – that is a universal panorama of every activity with no word to mark the people shown as Greeks. Virgil's shield depicts the history of Rome and that history is one of war. Rome is attacked and defended: Horatius keeps the bridge; the Gauls are rebuffed from the Capitol. In the middle the battle of Actium takes pride of place: 'In the centre rages the god of war, embossed in iron; the ominous Furies look on; and Discord exults in her torn cloak, while Bellona, the goddess of war, follows her with bloodstained whip' (8.700-3). That is not only a proud but also a horrifying vision of Rome's past. It is the weight which Aeneas must carry on his shoulder.

In Aeneas' absence the Trojan camp is besieged (book 9). The boy Euryalus and his lover Nisus (their love is *pius*, virtuous, has said Virgil at 5.296) undertake a sortie by night, to break through the Italian ranks and send news to Aeneas. They are carried away by the ease with which they kill sleeping enemies and Euryalus cannot resist taking a golden helmet from one of his victims. Its glint gives him away; he is caught and killed. Nisus, who could have got clear, vainly offers his own life to save his beloved and finally dies avenging him. The episode moved the poet greatly. It is striking that Homer never alludes to homosexuality, and Euryalus, who seems to be about fourteen, is younger than anybody in whom Homer is interested. The *Aeneid* is pervaded by beautiful youths, most of whom are killed; the eye of the poet lingers on them with an almost amorous tenderness. Thus as Euryalus dies: 'The blood flowed over his fair limbs and his head fell on to his shoulder, as when a crimson flower withers and dies, cut down by the ploughshare, or when a poppy is weighed down with rain, its neck is weary and its head bows down' (9.434ff.; see also 10.185ff., 10.325ff.). It will be the bitterest grief for Aeneas that he eventually fails to protect one such young man, Evander's son Pallas, and is forced to kill another, the Etruscan Lausus. So profoundly is Virgil moved by the death of his lovers Nisus and Euryalus that he breaks out: 'Lucky pair! If my song has any power, you shall never be forgotten as long as Aeneas' house rules on the unshaken Capitol and the Roman Empire endures' (9.446-9). We seem to see him trying to put that essentially homosexual sensibility at the service of the patriotic purposes of his poem, even preferring to forget that Nisus ought to have gone on alone to warn Aeneas and avert general ruin.

Next day Turnus breaks into the Trojan camp. He is unstoppable and kills a number of individuals. Yet, in his berserk rage, he does not think to open the gates to let in his army. If he had done so, that would have been the end of the Trojans (9.757-9). This is the Turnus who in the Eleventh book lays an ambush but, in a fit of emotion, abandons it too soon (11.901-2) and the same who takes the wrong sword for his final duel with Aeneas (12.731). His irrational violence marks him out, despite his prowess, for defeat.

Virgil has the problem of keeping Turnus and Aeneas apart. For when they meet, Aeneas must win – a victory that will bring the end of the war. In the *Iliad* this problem had not existed, because the plot hinged upon Achilles' withdrawal from the fighting: he does not meet Hector until the end of the epic. In *Aeneid* 9 Aeneas is away recruiting allies. In 10 he returns and the poet removes Turnus from the battlefield by the strange device of having Juno create a false Aeneas out of mist. Turnus pursues this phantom onto a ship, which sets sail and carries the mortified Turnus, his opponent having disappeared, away to his home city. The episode looks forward to the magical events of the Italian epics and of Spenser's *Faerie Queene*. In 11 Turnus makes angry speeches in council and, as we have seen, goes off to lay an ambush which turns out to be abortive. At the beginning of 12 a decisive duel between him and Aeneas is finally arranged but Juturna, Turnus' sister, induces the Italians to break the truce and shoot at Aeneas during the preparations. The result is a general battle and great slaughter. It is only by marching in the end on the city of Latinus and threatening to destroy it that Aeneas forces Turnus to face him, fight and die. His death marks the end of the poem.

This skeleton of events is deftly concealed, overlaid by the constant play of lively episodes. The Tenth book opens with a scene of dispute among the gods, Venus and Juno each passionately urging her case to Jupiter. Here, too, there is a difficulty, as the enormous superiority of Jupiter to the other gods and the clarity of his purpose make it hard to understand why he allows this terrible war in defiance of his own will. It was fundamental to Virgil's plan that the *Aeneid* should contain great battles, that the founding of Rome should be seen as laborious and also morally painful, since the Italians are to be part of Rome and the struggle has much of the horror of a civil war. As the poet himself asks – a question wrung from him by his suffering at the spectacle:

> tanton placuit concurrere motu,
> Iuppiter, aeterna gentis in pace futuras?

(A 12.503-4)

Was it your pleasure, Jupiter, that nations who were to live
together in unending peace should clash in such violence?

Again, as at 1.11, the poignant question remains unans-
wered. The will of Jupiter is not only benevolent but also
dark. From an analytic point of view, we can see that Virgil
is combining the old personal Zeus of Homer, whose will is
not necessarily moral or benign, with a more philosophical
conception of the supreme god, working out on earth his
purpose for the best. What Virgil makes of this is not, as it
might have been, a contradiction but, rather, a complex
unity which reflects the complexity of Roman history itself,
at once magnificent and terrible. So Jupiter allows the war
to go on, saying: 'The exertions of each side will bring them
their suffering and success. King Jupiter is the same to all.
Destiny will find a way' (10.111-13).

The great events of the Tenth book are the death of Pallas
and the death of Lausus. The dashing son of Evander, com-
mitted by his father to Aeneas' care, performs great exploits
and is killed by Turnus. 'I wish his father were here to watch',
says Turnus (10.443); and he strips from the body Pallas'
embroidered baldric – a gesture which will seal his own doom.
The slaying of Lausus is no less pathetic. He and Pallas are
of the same age and both are:

> egregii forma, sed quis Fortuna negarat
> in patriam reditus.

(10.435)

Outstanding in beauty, marked out by Fortune never to
return home.

The high-spirited and handsome young Lausus is the son
of the cruel and godless Etruscan king Mezentius, driven

into exile by the justified hatred of his people. The son rescues his unworthy father from Aeneas' attack. Aeneas shouts at him to withdraw and not force a single combat with an opponent too strong for him. However, the young man is carried away and Aeneas drives his sword through the tunic, which his mother had woven with gold thread (10.818). The boy dies and Aeneas is harrowed by the sight of his pale face and equally by the thought that, like himself, this youth was *pius*. Lausus' intimidated companions hang back and Aeneas picks up the body and calls to them to take it. We see the tableau, heavy with symbolic force, of the hero sighing heavily and holding in his arms the corpse of the charming boy whom he has had to kill: 'His neatly ordered hair clotted with blood' (10.832). The death of Dido, the shooting of the tame stag, the killing of Lausus – the same repeated pattern of destruction, not willed but still performed. That is an inseparable part of imperialism.

In the Eleventh book the morale of the Italians begins to crack, after a disastrous first day of fighting. There are angry scenes in Latinus' council but, despite the efforts of Aeneas, it proves impossible to stop the war. This book is marked by the episode of Camilla, a fighting maiden with a following of others like herself. A glamorous figure, she achieves great successes on the Italian side until an ignoble foe contrives to hurl a spear at her unseen – another pathetic death: 'The spear passed under her exposed breast and stuck deep, drinking her virgin blood.... Bloodless she fell; her eyes chilled and swam in death and the red colour left her cheeks.' (11.803, 818).

The Twelfth book opens with old Latinus begging Turnus to give up the struggle and renounce his hopes of Lavinia. The fiery young man, of course, refuses. Lavinia (who never speaks a word in the poem) blushes (12.64ff.) and we are given just a hint that she would have preferred Turnus. It is important that Aeneas is not to expect much human happiness from his union with this very young princess. At the end of the *Odyssey* Penelope is won by Odysseus, who kills the suitors to regain her. There it is made clear, by the subtle development of their encounter in *Odyssey* 23, that she is the appropriate and worthy wife for him, very like him in her powers of self-control and of deceiving others. There will be no such union between the middle-aged Aeneas and youthful Lavinia – a fact underlined when her mother, Queen Amata, hangs herself in despair at the thought of Aeneas marrying her daughter (12.593ff.). We remember from Jupiter's programmatic speech (1.283ff.) that, in fact, Aeneas is to live for only three more years. Humanly, he has had to surrender everything.

In the end, after all the diversions and delays, Aeneas and Turnus come face to face. As they fight on earth, a scene of reconciliation takes place in heaven. Jupiter finally tells Juno that her opposition must cease: 'I forbid you to meddle further' (12.806). She knows that destiny plans victory and immortality for Aeneas, that she has already been allowed to do her worst, that she must finally submit. She implores Jupiter at least to spare the Italian peoples the shame of having to change their name, their language or their dress: let them not become Trojans:

sit Romana potens Itala virtute propago.

(*A* 12.827)

Let Italian hardihood make Rome great.

This picks up a theme which has been touched on elsewhere in the poem – the moral character of the Italian people. A powerful speech in the Ninth book points a contrast between the effeminate Phrygians, with curled hair, music and womanish dress, and the toughness of the Italian peasantry: 'We spend all our lives in arms, drive on the ploughing ox with the butt of the spear...press down our grey hair with the

weight of the helmet...' (9.598ff.). All this recalls the sturdy
yeomen of the *Georgics* (*G* 2.472). Not, of course, that Aeneas
is effeminate or musical; but a contemporary Roman would
have had little respect for the contemporary people from the
Troad, the source of ecstatic cults; and Virgil, who wastes
nothing, exploits that prejudice too. The Trojan strain must
surrender something. Italy is not merely conquered; it has
a vital contribution to make.

Jupiter consents with a smile. The name of Troy shall
disappear and all shall henceforth be Latins – a people of
mixed blood who shall exceed both men and gods in *pietas*:

> hinc genus Ausonio mixtum quod sanguine surget
> supra homines, supra ire deos pietate videbis...
>
> (*A* 12.838-9)

They shall honour Juno most highly and that contents the
goddess, who smiles for the first time in the poem and aban-
dons Turnus to his doom. The scene is worth a moment's
reflection – not only the chilling sacrifice of Turnus by the
goddess who originally stirred him up to fight but also the
statement that Rome will actually outdo the gods in virtue.
What can it mean?

We get a hint in what immediately follows. Jupiter sends
a loathsome creature, winged and snaky, to paralyse Turnus'
will and nerve: two such horrid Furies, we read, sit at the
threshold of the cruel king (*Iovis ad solium saevique in limine
regis* [12.849]). It is recognised by Turnus' sister Juturna,
who has been ravished by Jupiter and in requital made
immortal. In bitterness and despair she cries: 'I recognise
the haughty commands of lofty Jupiter. Is this what he gives
me in exchange for my maidenhead? Why has he given me
eternal life? Why can I not die with my brother?' (12.876-
84). It is not easy to imagine the Jupiter whom we see in the
Aeneid, a grand and dispassionate deity, ravishing nymphs
in this off-hand way but the prominence of the idea at such

a crucial point in the poem seems designed to make us meditate on the morality of the great god who has just settled everything in so imposing a manner. We are reminded of another odd moment, in the Fourth Book. When Aeneas was living happily with Dido at Carthage, Jupiter was called on to intervene by an African prince whose love Dido had scorned. This man, Iarbas by name, turns out to be Jupiter's son 'by the rape of an African nymph' and he appeals to the god as his father (4.198ff.). Jupiter's rebuke is brought to Aeneas by Mercury:

> tu nunc Karthaginis altae
> fundamenta locas pulchramque uxorius urbem
> exstruis?
>
> (*A* 4.265-7)

> Are you now laying foundations for the towers of Carthage,
> and, like a husband, building a fine city?

'Like a husband' —Aeneas is bitterly taunted with his love for Dido. The taunt comes ill, he might have replied, from a supreme god who has himself treated a local nymph with much less ceremony and who now demands of the hero a virtue which exceeds that of the gods. In both places Virgil need not have employed this motif, since Jupiter must intervene and Turnus must die in any case. By employing it he remains, on the surface, within the conventions of mythical verse, in which the peremptory loves of gods for mortal women were legion. Yet in the pregnant atmosphere of the *Aeneid* the reader is encouraged to speculate on the justice of heaven and the hardness of a divine will which does indeed demand of the Romans a standard higher, in some ways, than it chooses to accept for itself.

Aeneas wounds Turnus and brings him to the ground. Turnus admits defeat, resigns his claim to Lavinia and begs for his life. Aeneas hesitates, standing over him with sword in hand ('More and more was Turnus' speech beginning to prevail on him'), when he sees round Turnus' chest the baldric he had stripped from the body of Pallas. Reminded of his grief – 'burning with fury and fearsome in his rage' – he kills him. The poem ends with the words: 'Turnus' body went cold and limp; his life fled lamenting to the shades below'.

That is a disquieting conclusion. Virgil could easily have made Turnus simply receive a deadly wound in the duel. Instead he makes it clear that Aeneas might have let him live but, in fact, killed him in an access of passion. *Parcere subiectis*, he was told in the Sixth book ('spare the defeated'). Romans were aware, at least in theory, that war should not be conducted in an irrational spirit of violence. Cicero has some eloquent pages on the subject; but Virgil perhaps saw more deeply when he created this scene. Killing has its own logic and war is not, in truth, compatible with calm rationality. We must remember that Turnus had it coming to him, that Pallas' father, old Evander, had demanded vengeance from Aeneas for his son (11.176ff.). Again Aeneas is pushed into an act of destruction which he might have preferred to avoid but the act remains upsetting, especially so because it forms the end of the poem. Virgil expects us to remember that Achilles slew Hector in *Iliad* 22, and that the killing was followed by nearly 2,000 lines of verse, in which the hero came to terms with the other Achaeans, with Hector's father and with the idea of his own approaching death. The *Aeneid*, by contrast, ends with a violent discord. Virgil cannot have intended to write a poem in thirteen or fourteen books. The Twelfth is, in fact, the longest in the *Aeneid*. It is not a mark of incompleteness that it ends where it does. The effect, haunting, complex and in harmony with the rest of the poem, is deliberate.

★ ★ ★ ★ ★

This account has emphasised the ambiguity of the *Aeneid* on central questions of Roman history and the nature of imperial power. That is not to say that the poem is anti-imperialist. There are resounding statements of the universal claims of Rome and they are not to be played down. 'Empire without limit I have given them', says Jupiter in the First book. Apollo predicts: 'The house of Aeneas shall rule the whole world – and their sons' sons, and those who are born of them' (3.97f.). The destiny of Rome, says Jupiter, is to put the whole world under its laws (*totum sub leges mitteret orbem* [4.231]; see also 6.781f., 7.98ff. and 8.998ff.). Rome will bring to the world the great Roman monosyllables – *pax*, *ius*, *mos*, *lex* (peace, justice, order, law) but she will do so by force. The unborn heroes whom Aeneas sees in the Underworld are a series of conquerors and the fate of Greece is to be a harsh subjection, which will avenge their destruction of Troy: 'The Trojans shall hold down famous Mycenae in slavery and rule over conquered Argos', says Jupiter (1.284-5). Anchises points out the unborn general Mummius with the words: 'He shall drive his chariot in triumph to the high Capitol, having conquered Corinth, famous for his slaughter of Greeks; he shall destroy Argos and Mycenae, city of Agamemnon...' (6.836-8). On the shield of Aeneas we see the figure of Augustus, seated in the temple of Apollo on the Palatine, receiving the tribute of a conquered world:

> He, seated in Apollo's shining temple, accepts the gifts of the nations and hangs them in the haughty portals. In they come, the vanquished peoples in long procession, as various in language as in dress and equipment. Here come the Nomads and the Africans in flowing robes, here the Lelegians and Carians and Gelonians with their bows and arrows...the Euphrates is humbled, and the Rhine, and the untamed Scythians, and the Araxes which flows into the Caspian Sea.
>
> (8.720ff.)

Such language and such images endorse the fullest claims of Roman imperialism.

It would have been easy, though perhaps not for Virgil, to produce a straightforward poem containing nothing but such sentiments. If that were what we had instead of the *Aeneid*, there would no longer be great interest in it now that it has, after all, turned out that the Roman Empire was not the last word of history. It is also not hard to produce literature which simply denounces aggrandisement, imperialism and war. We see such works nowadays in vast quantities. What Virgil has attempted to do is to deal justly with both sides. The ascendancy of Rome is an astonishing fact, inexplicable without divine favour. Rome will bring to the world the benefits of good and orderly administration. Thanks to Augustus, the Empire has emerged from a dark time, radiant with health and promise. Yet the cost has been tremendous. To have been singled out for that destiny has meant that the people of Rome have had to renounce the enticing delights of art, of beauty, even of love. They have had to become the agents of a providence which is little interested in their pleasures or even their happiness. But the 'arts' of conquest and dominion must be fit to stand beside the fine arts, which meant so much to Virgil as a man – and of which his epic is itself such a noble monument – and fit to stand as a historic destiny worthy of a great people.

To convey the complexity of his feelings and his message, Virgil created a style, unique in ancient literature, which is systematically capable of ambiguity. We can trace this up the scale, from single lines to the whole work. Thus when Aeneas has been ordered by the gods to forsake Carthage and Dido:

> ardet abire fuga dulcisque relinquere terras.
>
> (*A* 4.281)
>
> He burned to be gone in flight and to leave that sweet land.

The hero is on fire – to run away; he longs to leave the land whose sweetness he still feels. When battle is joined:

> primus turmas invasit agrestes
> Aeneas.

(*A* 10.310)

Aeneas was the first to attack the rustic columns.

Naturally the hero is first into the fray; but his victims are rustics – the very countrymen of the *Eclogues* and *Georgics*.

On a slightly larger scale, at the opening of the Seventh book Aeneas' old nurse Caieta dies, is buried and has a place named after her:

> tu quoque litoribus nostris, Aeneia nutrix,
> aeternam moriens famam, Caieta, dedisti;
> et nunc servat honos sedem tuus, ossaque nomen
> Hesperia in magna, si qua est ea gloria, signat.

(*A* 7.1-4)

You too, Caieta, by your death gave undying fame to our coasts; even now your resting-place is preserved by your story, and your name distinguishes your bones in mighty Italy, if that is any glory.

A mere etymology, not of the most interesting kind ('why is Cape Caieta so called?'), is coloured with emotion – first patriotic ('our coasts', 'mighty Italy') and confident ('undying fame'), then dying away into doubt and resignation ('is that really glorious?'). There is a perspective in which it is insignificant – the perspective of *Georgic* 2.497ff. and of philosophy.

We have already seen that the parade of Roman heroes at the end of the Sixth book is an example, on a substantial scale, of a similar technique – a virtuoso intertwining of positive optimism with pathos and despair. The story of Dido is yet larger. Aeneas is right to leave her; for the establishment of Rome is the overriding aim of the poem and of history. Yet neither Aeneas nor we can feel happy about her suffering and ruin; for the hasty departure of the hero from her shores is unedifying. Finally the whole poem, with its interplay of moods and directions – the story of a triumphant career which opens with the hero wishing he were dead and ends with him forced to kill a helpless opponent in a storm of passionate rage – is itself an example of this calculated ambiguity. In mathematics the combination of a plus and a minus is self-cancelling, leaving nothing; but an artist, if he is skilful enough, can find another, more mystical, mathematics in which that is not true. It is Virgil's achievement to have done that and so to have left us a work of inexhaustible inwardness – the greatest of all achievements of the creative mind of Rome and the truest interpretation of her history.

Chapter 5

Posthumous career and influence

The *Aeneid* was keenly anticipated by contemporaries. We have seen that the Emperor Augustus expressed anxiety to be shown even an unfinished sketch or a fragment. The poet Propertius announced the epic's imminence: 'Make way, you writers of Greece and Rome; something greater than the *Iliad* is on the way'. It was in the generation of Virgil and Horace that for the first time contemporary poetry began to be taught in schools and Virgil's works have remained a schoolbook ever afterwards, to the end of classical antiquity and far beyond, to the present day. The education of a Roman child, in fact, began with Virgil. The walls of Pompeii bear dozens of graffiti of Virgilian lines and tags, written before the destruction of that city in the great eruption of AD 79. In the first century AD Virgil is *the* poet, constantly quoted and echoed by almost every Latin writer, and receiving the ultimate accolade of universal familiarity, even made the subject of indecent burlesques. The epic poet Silius Italicus, an aristocrat and a wealthy man (his epic on the Punic War, surprisingly, survives – all seventeen books of it), not only imitated Virgil in his verse but bought his estate and held annual celebrations on his birthday. The much better epic poet Statius ends his epic on the Theban War by addressing his poem and telling it not to try to rival 'the divine *Aeneid*', but to reverence its footsteps from afar. Virgil was regarded with patriotic pride as the Roman counterpart to Homer; his style was the model for verse, as that of Cicero was for prose. There was an attempt in the time of Hadrian to revolt from the supremacy of these classic authors and to reinstate archaic writers such as Ennius in verse and the Elder Cato in prose but that proved a transient fashion. In fact, the dominance of Cicero and the Augustan poets was so complete that it led to the eclipse and eventually to the disappearance of the works of most earlier writers.

In the fourth century AD massive works of scholarship came into existence, expounding and interpreting Virgil's text. These works, by Servius, Macrobius and Donatus, preserve many remains of earlier scholarship, along with prolix and sometimes bizarre discussions from later periods. By the sixth century AD, with the progressive collapse of the old high culture, we find educated men described as having been instructed 'in the works of Virgil and in the law code'. Grammar was learned out of Virgil's text and the poet became, in many minds, more or less identified with grammar itself: an uncouth grammarian in Toulouse in the sixth century AD himself took the name P. Vergilius Maro and that is the only name by which we know him. For a barely literate age it was natural to connect literacy with uncanny power 'Grammar' shaded into 'grammarye' – a word for magic ('glamour', another word derived from 'grammar', had originally the same meaning). So Virgil became a great magician in the Dark Ages, famous for having made a bronze fly which protected Naples against all other flies, for preventing Vesuvius from erupting, balancing the city on an egg and so forth. The early Middle Ages could pay no higher compliment to a 'great clerk'.

Such was the prestige of Virgil and so universally familiar was his poetry, that it became a custom to open his works at random and select a line blindfold to serve as a guiding omen or as a prediction of the future (*sortes Vergilianae*). The future Emperor Hadrian, before his adoption by Trajan, was said to have drawn from the *Aeneid* a prediction of his elevation (6.805ff.). Savonarola, deciding to renounce business in favour of the church, drew on *Aeneid* 3.44: 'Flee far from the heartless shore, the land of avarice!'. It was said that Charles I, at the opening of the Civil War, drew on Dido's curse on Aeneas (4.615ff.): 'May he be harassed in war by a daring people, driven from his country, torn from the arms of his son, begging for aid and seeing the sad deaths of his friends. Even when he has accepted the terms of an unequal peace may he not enjoy his kingdom but die before his time and lie unburied'. In lighter vein, the young Horace Walpole claimed to have consulted Virgil on the character of George II and to have drawn on *Aeneid* 3.620: 'You gods, drive such a monster from the earth!'.

It was a lively question in the early Church whether the works of pagan writers should be studied by the faithful or rejected as idolatrous. Some rigorists tried to proscribe Virgil and Cicero ('You are a Ciceronian, not a Christian!' God thundered at St Jerome in a dream). They failed. St Augustine in his *Confessions* is tormented by the thought that as a boy he was more moved by the fictitious tragedy of Dido than by the real sufferings of his Saviour. Christian poets, like Prudentius, exploited Virgil to the full and he was never ousted from the school curriculum. It was natural that attempts should be made to reconcile him with the true faith. The Fourth *Eclogue*, with its prediction of a child saviour, especially the phrase *iam redit et Virgo* ('now the Virgin returns') seemed to mark him out as a prophet and early in the fourth century a Christian interpretation of the poem was officially laid down and universally accepted. The presence of Virgil in the *Divine Comedy* of Dante and the presence in the Sistine Chapel of the Sibyls, all of whom have received Christian prophetic status thanks to the Sibyl of the *Eclogue*, go back ultimately to this source. The tender soul of Virgil might indeed seem 'naturally Christian'. Soon the story sprang up that St Paul had wept at Virgil's tomb and said:

'What I would have made of you, had I found you alive!'. In the darkest period, when all notions of accurate chronology were lost, stories were told of Virgil actually being a Christian; attempting even, anachronistically, to convert none other than the Emperor Nero.

In the work of the poets of the Carolingian revival, during the late eighth to the tenth centuries, the influence of Virgil is omnipresent. Apart from echoes, quotations and allusions, we possess an epic poem (*Waltharius*) by the cleric Ekkehard, which tells an episode from the time of Attila the Hun in lively Virgilian verse. Dante was steeped in Virgil and in the *Divine Comedy* hailed him as his master and teacher, the source of 'the fine style that has won me honour'. No higher compliment was ever paid by one great poet to another than this opening address and the choice of the noble pagan as his guide through Hell and Purgatory – not Virgil the grammarian's favourite nor Virgil the wizard, but Virgil the clear-sighted poet of empire and of human life.

The Renaissance saw the production of hundreds of poems in Latin, which were as Virgilian in technique as the humanists who wrote them could contrive, from Petrarch's epic *Africa* to the *Eclogues* of Mantuan and Sannazaro, even to Fracastoro's *Syphilis, or the French Disease*, in which that unappealing subject is treated with urbanity and liveliness in Virgilian hexameters. These works were highly esteemed in their time – 'Ah, good old Mantuan...old Mantuan, old Mantuan! Who understandeth thee not, loves thee not,' croons the pedantic schoolmaster in *Love's Labours Lost* – but nowadays they interest only specialists. The influence of Virgil was not confined to Latin. The pastoral in all European languages depended on emulation of the *Eclogues*; the first opera to be written and produced in modern Europe, at the ducal court of Mantua, was on the Virgilian theme of Orpheus and Eurydice. Purcell's *Dido and Aeneas* is certainly one of the greatest pieces of music composed in

England; Gluck's *Orfeo ed Euridice* and Berlioz' *Les Troyens* stand beside it as works inspired by Virgil. The Italian epic of Tasso on the liberation of Jerusalem by the Crusaders, the Portuguese national epic of Camõens, Milton's *Paradise Lost* – all rely on the Virgilian model and the Virgilian style. Milton has the full epic equipment, even to the opening invocation of the 'heavenly Muse', the long similes, the scenes of debate and of battle. Above all, perhaps, the long sentences and organised paragraphs of his poem, which testify to the poet's own intellectual and architectonic power, owe much to the elaborate but ordered periods of Virgil. In defence of his own subject Milton calls it:

> Sad task, yet argument
> Not less but more Heroic than the wrauth
> Of stern *Achilles* on his Foe pursu'd
> Thrice Fugitive about *Troy* wall; or rage
> Of *Turnus* for *Lavinia* disespous'd,
> Or *Neptun's* ire or *Juno's*, that so long
> Perplex'd the *Greek* and *Cytherea's* Son...
>
> (*Paradise Lost*, 9.14-19)

This is to say that *Paradise Lost* has not only the sublimity of revelation but also all (and even more) of that epic heroism which marked the *Iliad*, the *Odyssey* and the *Aeneid*.

Dryden translated the whole of Virgil and his prose writings quote Virgil and mention him more than any other writer, even Shakespeare. Milton's epic is highly serious but the burlesque epics of Pope, *The Rape of the Lock* and the *Dunciad*, are less Virgilian. Both these poems, in different ways the masterpieces of their author, presuppose familiarity in the reader with all the paraphernalia and the language of the classical epic. Later, in the eighteenth century, such meditative poems as Thomson's *The Seasons* followed in the footsteps of the *Georgics*. Tennyson was a great lover of Virgil and, at the request of the people of Mantua, he wrote a poem *To Virgil*, to celebrate the nineteenth centenary of the poet's birth:

I salute thee, Mantovano,
I that loved thee since my day began,
Wielder of the stateliest measure
Ever moulded by the lips of man.

In the twentieth century the greatest advocate of Virgil in the English-speaking world was T.S. Eliot. His influential essay *What is a Classic?*, which appeared in his book *On Poets and Poetry* (1951), went so far as to say that there could be only one classic in Europe and that was Virgil – central in history because of the significance of the Roman Empire itself, and uniquely civilised because of his attitude to power and to humanity. Such is the versatility of great literature that Mussolini, by contrast, subsidised the production of texts of Virgil and encouraged the reading of his works as incentives to a specifically Italian imperialism.

This brief sketch cannot hope to do more than give the barest outline of the continuing influence and importance of Virgil in western culture. The subject is so vast that it represents in itself a considerable part of the history of that culture; and many monographs have been written on it. It is my hope that this book may have helped to explain the continuing fascination of the work of a very great poet.

Further reading

The standard text of Virgil is the Oxford Classical Text edited by R.A.B. Mynors (not the old one edited by F.A. Hirtzel). That is the text quoted in this volume. There is a text with facing English prose translation by H.R. Fairclough in the Loeb Classical Library series. Dryden's translation is a great achievement, which in some respects conveys the feeling of the original, its rhetoric and splendour, better than any other. Dryden lived in a period which was saturated in the Latin classics and his own style was closer to theirs than that of any twentieth-century translator can be, though he is at times very far from the literal sense of the original and his rhyming couplets impose a different movement from that of Virgil's long periods. C. Day Lewis translated Virgil well into readable modern verse (Oxford, 1966; reprinted in The World's Classics as two paperback volumes: *Eclogues and Georgics*, with introduction and notes by R.O.A.M. Lyne, 1985; and *Aeneid* with introduction and notes by Jasper Griffin, 1986). There is a helpful, brief commentary on Day Lewis's translation of the *Aeneid* by R.D. Williams (Bristol Classical Press, 1985). There are good versions of the *Eclogues* by Guy Lee (Liverpool, 1980); of the *Georgics* by L.P. Wilkinson (Harmondsworth [Penguin], 1982) and Robert Wells (Manchester, 1982); and of the *Aeneid* by Robert Fitzgerald (London, 1984).

The poet's early life is well treated in the second chapter of L.P. Wilkinson, *The Georgics of Virgil* (Cambridge, 1969;

paperback from Bristol Classical Press, 1997). The historical and political background may be found in R. Syme's classic *The Roman Revolution* (Oxford, 1939).

There is a helpful introduction to Robert Coleman's edition of the *Eclogues* (Cambridge, 1977). L.P. Wilkinson's book on the *Georgics*, cited above, is the best on that poem. W.A. Camps, *An Introduction to Virgil's Aeneid* (Oxford, 1969) is an admirably compact short book on the *Aeneid*. Brooks Otis, *Virgil: A Study in Civilized Poetry* (Oxford, 1963) is more subjective – exciting but sometimes vulnerable. R.O.A.M. Lyne, *Further Voices in Vergil's Aeneid* (Oxford, 1986) deals with the 'polyphonic' composition of the poem. The sinister and daemonic side of the *Aeneid* is brought out by W.R. Johnson, *Darkness Visible* (California, 1976). There is a good collection of papers: *Virgil, A Collection of Critical Essays*, edited by S. Commager (Englewood Cliffs, N.J., 1966). Gordon Williams' *Tradition and Originality in Roman Poetry* (Oxford, 1968) illuminates many passages in Virgil and in other authors. Domenico Comparetti, *Vergil in the Middle Ages* (English translation, 1895; reprinted, 1966), contains much curious information. There are two recent books on Virgil's influence: R.D. Williams and T.S. Pattie, *Virgil: His Poetry through the Ages* (London, 1982), well illustrated; and Charles Martindale (editor), *Virgil and His Influence* (Bristol Classical Press, 1984), on the debt to him of later poets and artists – both available in paperback.

On *Aeneid* 1, 2, 4 and 6 there are commentaries by R.G. Austin; on 3 and 5 by R.D. Williams; on 7 and 8 by C.J. Fordyce (all originally Oxford University Press, though the last three volumes are now available from Bristol Classical Press); also on 8 by K.W. Gransden (Cambridge University Press, 1976). R.D. Williams has published a short commentary on the whole of the *Aeneid* (originally Macmillan/ Nelson, London, 2 vols., 1972, now available from Bristol Classical Press).

Index